I0408804

When I was Mikey

A story of resiliency

By Whip Rawlings

*I*t was April 11th 2004,

I returned to Indianapolis Indiana to retrieve some clothes from my daughter's house that I left there during my last trip. I made a point to visit my oldest sister and my father. My sister Sherry was plagued by lupus, a crippling disease and my father was a sickly man with one foot in the grave, he survived two triple heart bypass surgeries and a stroke.

I have not seen or talked to him in five years, and this would be the first time I purposely sat down to have a meaningful conversation with him during my life time. I felt a need to have closure even if it meant I had to forgive him. My father was uneducated and igno- rant. I guess his ignorance and low self-esteem kept him from progressing beyond the sixth grade, he didn't care about anything or anyone around him, not even himself. His physical health was rapidly deteriorating as a result of no physical activity and his un- healthy eating habits. He had every aging physiological failure known to man, diabetes, high blood pressure, congestive heart failure, and other aging ailments not yet discovered. My father grew up in a lower social economic class, and the only positive role models he could relate to farmers or general laborers, he felt that being a gangster was his only way out of poverty.

My father was a short, stocky, and strong man. His shoulders favor that of a football player and his thighs were big like a professional wrestler. By the time he was 50 he had just about wither down to nothing, his broad shoulders sagged down like wet sponges. His muscular thighs were that of shaved chicken legs. His cast-iron frame was just a weaker shell of the person he once was. His eating habits were very poor, his daily meal consisted of pig feet and a bowl of cornflakes floating in sugar. His eating habits was pushing him towards a grave quick, fast and in a hurry. I did not know if I would get another chance to hear him say.

"I'm sorry for not being a father to you."

I knew I had to see him before I returned to Sacramento. I asked my mother if she knew my father's address and phone number. She abruptly sprang from her chair and dashed up the stairs to her bedroom, where she dug through a stack of miscellaneous papers. She returned one minute later and handed me a piece an of paper revealing his address. I jumped into my rental car then drove west on 10th St. across the once grand metal bridge that stood over White River.

I pulled slowly up to the front of his house. I sat in the car and pondered about what I was going to say to him and how I was going to approach the situation. Violent visions ran rapidly through my mind. I had thoughts of kicking in the door, bum rushing him, forcing him to the floor, forcing him to apologize for disappearing for 18 years of my childhood. I wanted to make him pay for being an absentee father, I didn't want money, I needed a coup de grace. I spent many years in the military and was trained how to hurt and kill people but it wasn't in my heart to hurt anyone, even someone who purposely abandoned me during my greatest time of need, during the most impressionable time of my life. But the thought of attacking him was inescapable in my mind.

After running the thought of extirpating him back and forth through my mind for several more minutes, I stepped out of my car assured. I walked up his driveway then towards the side entrance to his door. As I approached the door I noticed my father walking past the door, taking short choppy steps as though he just had another stroke. He looked very weak and disheveled, with an unwashed T-shirt, homemade cut off shorts and a worn out pair of slippers.

He slowly walked as he dragged his feet carrying his dishes to the sink, this was the moment I'd held in my subconscious for 42 years, and this was the moment I rehearsed in the waking hours of my restless nights. I slowly walked up to door, prowling like a tiger about to pounce on fresh meat, I snatched the screen door open and quickly stepped into the kitchen catching him completely off guard. I looked at him with a stern look and said.

"What's my name?"

He replied "Mikey".

I was totally amazed, even in his weak condition, for the first time in 30 years he had gotten my name right. He usually called me Denton, my brothers name and I spent the first 30 years of my life correcting him.

The fact that he actually got my name right for the first time in the history of my life helped to deflate the anger I was ready to unleash on him.

"I need to talk to you about something, about my childhood and what I went through because you decided not to be a part of my life".

Instead I sat patiently waiting to hear those words (I'm sorry son) but he never uttered a word, he didn't even provide an explanation for his being an absentee parent.

He could barely talk or acknowledge anything I said, the stroke left his voice impaired, and his once strong cast iron frame was now just a shell of a man I once knew. I told my father of the hard times I had growing up without his financial and physical support. How I used card board to line the bottom of my shoes to keep snow from entering the holes on the soles of my shoes. And how I kept his birthday card I couldn't send to him because I never knew where he lived. Tears fell from his eyes as I recounted my economical dilemmas enhanced by his absence. But I soon realized that his tears were from his sickness and not from listening to my past cries for fatherly love.

I explained to my father that I was only three years old when he was arrested. I described everything he wore as he sat in the back of the police car hand cuffed. He wore a London fog trench coat and a black fedora hat. I was only a toddler but the incident was so emotionally traumatic it burnt an impression in my mind that I would carry the rest of my life.

"Come on, I want to show you something" he said.

As he lead me into his bedroom I realized that his life has come to this, a rented room with torn curtains, a broken down bed shoved in the corner without a frame, lying squarely on the floor, an empty safe where he kept his life possessions. A timex watch of little value, a seven diamond cluster ring and a news articles of himself in the back seat of a police car being arrested after an unsuccessful bank heist. My father was sixty-seven years old and his only claim to fame was a foiled Bank robbery.

I don't expect or want anything from him other than an apology and a chance to forgive him. He played his best hand in life and by doing so he played himself. After waiting forty-four years to hear my father say.

"Son, I am sorry"

Was no longer necessary, his life circumstance apologized for his uncaring, thoughtless, selfish behavior. Although I am not extremely pleased with the downward spiral of my father's life. I wish he had been more an auspicious part of my life. Our two hour bonding session had come to an abrupt end but before I left I asked for a hug, this would be my first hug from my father in forty four years, and then I said,

"Dad I forgive you for what happened in our past".

At that very moment I felt the tension in my shoulders loosen, my shoulders slumped down to a relaxed position, it felt as if 100 pounds of hate, that had been haunting my soul for more then 40 years, released and I instantly felt revised. I closed this chapter of hate in my life, and opened a chapter of forgiveness for my dad. I returned to my mother's house and sat on the front porch recounting my pass childhood experiences.

I was born on a cold windy December morning in 1959 at 4 AM. It was the year of the pig, the temperature high for the year was 50° and the low was 39°. Sam the rhesus monkey was launched into space from Wallops Island Virginia. The Barbie doll went on sale, debut 8 million sold. The first weather satellite was launched. US president Dwight Eisenhower signed Hawaii in the statehood. The Dalai Lama fled China and was granted political asylum in India. Cuba invaded Panama. Benjamin O. Davis Jr became the first black Major General in the US Air Force. America's new 49 star flag honoring Alaska statehood unfurled. The Lincoln Memorial design on the US penny went into circulation. The total snowfall for the year was 5.20 inches.

I was blessed with a long-term memory that stretches back more than 55 years. In 1962 my mother repetitiously dressed me in a blue sailor suit, I could recall when my brother Dale died in 1962, and a year later my little sister was born in 1963. I could recall my grandfather's tall lanky 6'3 thinner then a rail frame. His head was covered with gray straight hair and the smell of his pipe reeked throughout the house. I recall the times I watched him shave with a straight razor and the day he killed his rooster with an axe because the rooster chased my sister around the yard and pecked her on the leg. I was born into the world without a compass. I landed on my destination of being born a mischievous kid, thrust down the river of a life of excitement and uncertainty without a paddle.

My mother always said I was different from the rest of the children in my family, that I wasn't afraid to try new things and I enjoyed life to the fullest. By the time I arrived on the scene my mother had already given birth to five other siblings. She was a young 23-year-old girl, with a husband who couldn't seem to get his life together. My father was a hard worker I guess, sometimes I think the pressure of having another child was too much for him to contemplate. My mother was six months pregnant with me the day she decided to lie around the house and have a little time to herself.

She lay idling on the bed, reading a newspaper and out of nowhere my father came flying through the air diving on the bed barely missing my mother's stomach. Only her quick reflects saved me as she rolled out of his way. I would have been sent back to the ages if my mother hadn't roll over to one side preventing him from landing forcefully on her stomach ending my embryonic life. Although I don't have many good memories of my father or my early child hood, I was a very conscious child early in my life. Conscious enough to remember the first few years of my life seemed cold and empty.

I believe a difficult childhood makes for a really conscious child.

I must have been overly conscious, I remember everything. I remembered my mother often dressing me up and a blue sailor suit because she thought it was cute. I remember my father and mother not being at home very often. I don't remember my father picking me up or talking to me or hugging me. I only remember how distant I was from him, how cold and disengaged I was from the father son relationship. My father was far from being Andy Griffin, and my family is far from being a middle class nuclear family. Any one of my siblings could testify to how very little hugs or affection we received, mostly because I was the sixth child and got lost somewhere in the shuffle.

We were a family of six with one on the way. We had little money and our clothes and meals were statements of poverty not yet published. My life took off as if it was a pre-written story. The early drama I experience helped aide in the development of my long term memory. I was three and a half years of age when my first official accident occurred. What I mean by official, the incident was officially recorded as a medical and legal document.

My mother was out shopping late one evening, I wasn't sure of her whereabouts but that didn't deter me from taking full advantage of her absence, so I took the liberty of using her bed to play cowboys and Indians. My sisters didn't seem to care what I did as long as I didn't interrupt their routine of watching their favor programs on one of the three TV channels. Aluminum foil wrapped around the antenna and wire stretching to the window trying to pick up a clear reception.

"Another cowboy and Indian movie"

I thought to myself, It seemed to me the Cowboys always win in the movies and since I have 1% Chippewa Indian blood in me I was sure to make the Indians win this battle.

I began franticly jumping up and down on the bed while my siblings desperately tried to watch TV. Sherry would reach back and slap me on the leg as many times as it took to get me to quit jumping up and down, they stopped watching TV long enough to quiet me down by placing their hands over my mouth. Soon they would overpowered me by sitting on my back and my legs. I pretended I was hurt for a second and being the soft hearted girls they were they felt empathy for me and quickly jumped off my back and freed my legs. I laid on the bed idle for several minutes, But as soon as they were back watching their program, I returned to my jumping exhibition.

I decided an Indian couldn't possibly fight Cowboys without a weapon so I leaped from the bed losing my footing and almost knocking the TV off the cart. I ran to the kitchen, scrambled through a few draws and grabbed my weapon of choice. I looked admiringly at a fork and said.

"Those Cowboys are in for it now".

Back to the bedroom I ran, crawling over my sisters to get back to the imaginary battle-field. I was submerge deep into my fighting scene when I jumped too high in the air. My feet must have been 5 feet in the air. I began falling uncontrollably. As I landed, I totally missed the bed thereby landing on the floor.

The metal points on the fork were sticking straight in the air and drove their way deep into my right eyebrow stopping only after the entire fork was embedded in my head. As I lay motionless on the floor, my oldest sister Sherry said.

"Ha, ha, see what you get".

She wasn't yet aware of the trouble I was in. She thought I had just fell off the bed and bumped my head but I lay lifeless, pools of blood began to run profusely from my forehead until the blood touch my sister Tiana's finger. Tiana screamed.

"Mikey is bleeding!"

Sherry jumped to her feet screaming and crying for someone to call for help, Sherry's panic caused my other sisters to panic. It was total chaos, my face was saturated with blood, and I could see feet running back and forth while blood slowly blurred my vision.

Sherry kneeled down beside me trying her best to comfort me by patting me on the back and crying out loud.

"Someone please get help!"

I could no longer see past the blood streaming down my face but I could feel the uncertainly and the fear coming from my sisters pulsating hand gripping my arm. I began to slowly go into an unconscious state of mind, and eventually I blacked out. I was awakened by the pressure placed on my forehead by a tall white men, wearing a white uniform with broad shoulders trying to remove the fork from my head. The more he pulled on the fork, the more I kicked, yelled and screamed bloody hell for him to stop pulling. After three minutes of trying to remove the fork he couldn't take it anymore, he gave into my whining and screaming.

He said, " Let's go, they will have to remove the fork at the hospital".

Placing me on the gurney they pushed me down the steps into the ambulance. He re-assured me as I was placed into an old ambulance that resembled a funeral hearse. I was taken to Wishard Memorial Hospital less than three miles from my grandparents house. The siren screamed as the red lights illuminated the ground 10 feet in front and 5 feet on either side causing cars to move to one side of the road just for me. Once I ar-rived at the hospital, I was placed on a gurney and rushed immediately into the operat-ing room then strapped down on the table. A heavyset African-American woman pushed a silver tray next to my bed, displaying small gold hooks and syringes filled with a liquid substance, capped off with long dual needles. I just knew this wasn't for me, someone must have left it there by accident or forgot it and they would be back soon to claim it.

I couldn't believe what my eyes were seeing. The needles were as long as my arm. I recognized the hooks from my uncle George's bait and tackle box but I had no clue as to why the needles were there. A tall white gentleman wearing a long white coat stretching down to his knees entered the room. He gently palpated the orbital rim of my eye, I screamed bloody hell as he touched and applied pressure with his oversized fin-gers. I screamed and kicked until my mother and father were summoned into the oper-ating room. My mother did her best trying to hold my arms and my father held my legs down until they tightened up the loosely fitting bed straps over my legs.

"Hold his legs and arms down tight"

Once again the man in the white coat approached the right side of my bed holding the needle in the air, tiny drops of fluid leaked for the tip The doctor removed one of the long needles filled with a clear liquid substance from the cart. He didn't hesitate shoving the needle right into my eyebrow. I was so traumatized by the event I squirmed free from under the bed straps then slapped the needle from the doctor's hand.

"Hold his legs and arms down tight" The doctor said.

And that was the last thing I remember as I was fading asleep a grey square shaped cloth that resembles the cover of a 45 record with a hole in the middle was placed over my eye partially blocking my view of the tray on the right side of the bed filled with needles, hooks and thread. My mother was standing beside my hospital bed when I awoke; tears pierced her eyes as she looked at me shaking her head in disbelief. My father sat in the corner with his lips poked out and a swollen face as though he had been in a fight. The car ride home was anything but joyous. I sat in the front seat of the passenger side of the car wrapped in my mother's arms, my father was silent the entire trip, but if looks could kill, his look were so hard and so cold my sensitive side took over and I began to cry. After I arrived home my sisters were glad to see me, it was not long before they began teasing me and making jokes about my accident. Time passed and I watched my family regroup and return to our drama free lifestyle.

Three weeks had passed since the fork accident, My life returned to some sense of normalcy, boring mornings, watching my brothers and sisters get ready for school. My sister Sherry skipped school that morning because she was fighting the flu. Any other day my feisty behavior would be more than Sherry could handle, but due to the medication I was taking it left me groggy and off balance, cutting my energy level in half, making me a dull normal child. The house was empty and cold as though no one had ever lived there, with every step I could hear my footsteps echo down the empty hallway. Suddenly there was a loud banging noise at the back door. I wasn't allowed to answer the door, so I yelled for my big sister Sherry. The banging on the door intensified.

Sherry griped, moaned, groaned and complained as she climbed from her bed, placing her feet on the cold hardwood floor, she made her way to the kitchen door. I peaked around the corner and I could see the fear in Sherry's eyes as she slowly approached the back door. As I stood there I observe a tall white male wearing a blue suit with many Silver buttons alined down the front of his jacket, flanked by a metal badge on his chest and a metal badge on his hat.

He instructed Sherry to open the door, she nodded her head no.

She said "I'm not allowed to open the door for strangers".

 The police then instructed her to back away from the door, just as she moved away from the door. I ran toward the door dragging a chair behind me. I placed the chair at the door trying to get a view of what was going on, just as the policeman was about to crash through the door, he looked up and saw me peeking through window.

He came to a screeching halt smacking his shoulder against the frame of the door then yelling.

 "Pull that kid out of the way".

Just as Sherry reached up and grabbed me by the arm, pulling me from the chair the door exploded as if a bomb had gone off. Glass and broken wood flew past my freshly bandage eye. I broke free from my sister's grip and ran upstairs to search for my weapon. I made a quick search underneath the bed where I last saw my fork; the fork was nowhere to be found. So, I opened my dresser draw, digging frantically under a combination of mixed socks. I didn't find my fork but I found something more powerful. Something that will give me total control over the entire situation. I found my Superman ring at the bottom of a half eaten bag of Chesty potato chips.

I was in luck. I knew I could power up by placing the ring on my finger and holding it high in the air. I could fight these villains. So I hid behind the door waiting for the first sign of a blue suit lined with silver buttons. I could hear heavy footsteps approaching at a rapid pace from a distance in the hallway. By this time I was fully powered up and ready to save the day, as I've seen so many times on Batman and Robin. As the officer turned the corner. I sprung from behind the door grabbing onto the officer's leg. I tried lifting him in the air as if I was flying off, surprisingly, my feet began to take flight as though I was actually flying. By the time I was in mid-flight, I realized I was being held by the back of my shirt in midair. The officer looked at me while gasping to catch his breath. His gun was in his right hand with his finger wrapped around the trigger.

He stumbled and fell back against the wall still holding me in midair. He had a look in his eyes that was very familiar, it was the same look my father had given me only a week earlier while in the hospital. The officer lowered me to my feet and said.

"Don't ever do that again, you could've gotten hurt".

But once again I broke free from his clutches and sprinted down the wooden steps, dashing towards the front door. I could see my sister and my mother standing on the front porch, the men in the blue suit walked quickly past me out to his car with one red light flashing on the top of the car turning in a circle. There was someone sitting restlessly in the backseat of the police car with their hands bound behind them. I wanted to get a closer look, because maybe it was one of the villains I fight every day after I power up with my Superman ring.

I scurried closer to the car for a better view of the villain. The person became more recognizable the closer I got. He slowly turned his head towards me then stared straight into my eyes. I stumbled back and fell in the snow, my heart was beating like a rabbit being chased by a fox. It was my father! Still wearing the same trench coat and fedora hat he was wearing as he left for work this morning. I didn't understand, so I reach for the door handle of the car and pulled the door until it was slightly ajar. Before I knew it I was flung to the ground.

My mother yelled out frantically from the porch.

"Keep your damn hands off my son!"

My hand hit the ground so hard it shattered my plastic Superman ring. I was powerless. I didn't know what else to do. The officer slammed the door shut yelling.

" Stay away from the car and move back!"

I didn't know what else do, I reached around my mother to get one more look. I stood close to the car with my face pressed against the glass until it began to fog up. I drew a smiling face on the window just before the car drove off. My mother and I stood outside watching the patrol car as it turned the corner, and within seconds my father disappeared and I would not see him for another three years.

My father was on his way to prison for robbing a bank. This bright ideal of my father and his brothers left my mother alone to take care of six children, with one bun in the oven. My mother was unemployed prior to my father's incarceration. He left her penniless, powerless and unable to pay the rent.

Three weeks had passed and we found ourselves facing a new challenge, 'rent' was due and our support system was on his way to a federal prison for three to six years. Our furniture was tossed out onto the snow covered front yard and the doors were locked behind us. Tiana and I bundle up together trying to stay warm on a slightly damped snow covered couch. I was only three and a half years of age but I was no stranger to recognizing pain and uncertainty on my mother's face, she wanted to cry but she fought back her tears sparing us any discomfort and freeing us from worry.

$\mathcal{V}$alley Avenue

Within a weeks time we moved less than a half mile down the street to my fathers grandmother's double. A cozy little green double with concrete bricks separating the two front porch. There was one small problem, a tall strange looking black man was going from window to window looking inside our house. I've never seen this fool before and I had no way of defending myself. My Superman ring was broke and my weapon I used to fight the Cowboys with was placed out of my reach. This strange man wore a Dockers men's ear flap hat, also known as Elmer FUD hat, he also wore a checkered hunting jacket and black rubber snow boots that he never buckled up. Mother told us he's no one to fear, this is your uncle Robbie. Robbie was tall and slim, with huge lips flopping around like two uncooked pieces of baloney. Lips that only a mother could love. My father never spoke of Robbie because Robbie was mentally challenged which made him a source of embarrassment for my father.

I don't recall too much about this house other than it had huge sunflowers and Venus fly traps as tall as my grandfather in the backyard. I wasted no time testing the reflexes of the fly traps. I poked and prodded until my grandmother told me that the fly traps could eat me whenever they want. I don't know if I believed what she said was true or not. What I did know is I didn't have my power ring and I wasn't going to test that theory until I could power up again. Robbie was mentally challenged, but, I felt safe around him; he patrolled inside and outside the house several times a day, including late into the night.

I would catch him peeking through my bedroom window scaring us half to death. After several weeks we got use his antics and he just became another part of the landscape. He was very tender hearted and sensitive but very strong internally. He reminded me of the man that saved the little boy and girl in the movie To Kill a Mockingbird. He was a reclusive person. He never spoke, he only observed from a distance and acted as a protector of the house. I could tell that he loved us, although being mentally undeveloped he was unable to express his emotions clearly. The months hurried by, the spring turned into summer the summer to fall, time wasn't waiting for anyone neither was my unborn baby-sitter Denise, because she was pushing hard and overly eager to enter the New racially charged World.

Sheffield Street

My mother was very fortunate in some aspects of her life. She had a macro support system including two living parents and five sisters. Her parents didn't have much money, the only help she would get from her parents was their much needed love and the succor she needed for the moment. During her visit to the hospital they offered to tend to our needs while she delivered my little sister. We packed our bags and piled into my aunt's 1963 Buick Oldsmobile.

The car was brand-new, and despite having an adult son whom lived independent of her household, nevertheless she felt compelled to have plastic perfectly tailored to the car seats. We were fortunate that the ride was less than 20 minutes, because on a hot day you could dehydrate if you rode more than 30 minutes inside of that sauna on wheels. My grandparents lived in a small white turn-of-the-century clapboard house with Ionic style design on the front. The small Ft $800.^2$ home didn't even have a bathroom. The toilet was located in the backyard just like in the western movies, and we took baths in a large metal tub. I loved my grandparents but I could only deal with them three hours at a time, not for an entire week. We've never stayed with them in the past and they weren't aware of my physical shortcomings once I fell into a deep sleep.

They've never experienced the nocturnal monster (bed wetting) in their house and I didn't know how they will react once they saw the nocturnal monster occupy forbidden territory. The house was so small there was no escaping my grandparents not finding out about the nocturnal monster. The house was cramped with only two bedrooms, a front room, kitchen and a cellar in the kitchen floor. The house totally creeped me out. I could feel the presence of the prior tenants from the 1800s walking around the house in their ghostly figures. The wooden floors squeaked for no reason at all as if someone walked constantly around the house. The coterie of my family sat around the kitchen table filling the house with laughter as I sequester myself in the front room staring at the bowl of orange slice candy that permeated my every thought.

There were five of us, including my cousin Tommy and his mother, who also resided in the small house. My grandparents didn't seem to mind us moving in with them temporarily, at least they never spoke badly of us living with them out loud. I tried to be as inconspicuous as possible, staying out of their way, trying not to make our stay there any more difficult than it was, because I didn't want anything else bad to happen to my mother.

She had been through enough, putting up with my fathers antics and his laissez faire approach to raising kids. Her face was flushed from pain and fear but at the same time, I could see determination in her eyes. Although her parents were only able to provide minimal financial support, she wasn't alone. Her sister Dorothy provided transportation whenever she could and Dorothy's husband George occasionally dropped by to deliver a box of day-old donuts from his job at a local bakery. It often made him feel good when he threw a hand full of coins in the air and watched us scramble around the floor gathering his loose change.

I couldn't have imagine how my mother felt, nor could I imagine the uncertainty she was feeling. How could my father make this unilateral decision without considering his children? How could he leave us in dire straits? There was a huge question hovering over my head, an empty void that I had to find someway to fill. How was she going to make it without the support of another income, without the strength of our father? How long would it take, before we wore out our welcome at our grandparent's house. While my brothers and sisters played in the front yard with our cousins, I sat on the porch staring down the street in anticipation of my mother turning the corner any minute.

There I waited day in and day out. Once again I was distracted by the large glass candy bowl filled with orange slices that set centered on the front room table taunting me from a distance. The top was made of a thin metal that made a pinging sound anytime someone try to remove the top. This kept me occupied for hours on end, but once I realize I couldn't remove the candy from the bowl without getting caught, I went back onto the front porch and watched for my mother. I was hoping she would turn the corner any minute, just seeing her would make everything all right in my mind. We just lost our father, now our mother is missing in action.

I knew she was having a baby but I thought a huge bird would deliver it to our house. So I searched the sky with my eyes, looking for a huge stork with a baby hanging from its beak.

"Why are you looking at the sky boy?". My grandmother said.

"I'm looking for my little sister, isn't she going to be delivered by a large stork" I said,

With a puzzled look on my face. My grandmother kissed me on the forehead, laughing to herself she walked back in the house.

I love my grandparents, especially my grandmother because she made the best baloney sandwiches on the planet. She took her time when she smeared the sandwich spread on the bread and delicately placed a piece of cheese with an unfamiliar taste right between the mayonnaise and the baloney. Then she cut the sandwich in two triangular pieces and wrapped it in wax paper. But I missed my mom because I depended on her for everything, and besides my grandmother wasn't a part of my microsystem, someone I'd depended on for life not just for an occasional great tasting bologna sandwich.

I went to bed wondering where my mother was and how she was doing. I could barely eat my dinner or hold a single thought in my head. Although I've visited my grandparents many times, I still was not use to sleeping in a strange bed. The rules of their house were much different them my own home. We all had to take baths, one at a time, in a steel bathtub placed in the center of kitchen, my grandmother boiled pot after pot of hot water. It was a tedious and a never ending process. I sat quietly in the front room watching my sister's file in and out of the kitchen. While my grandmother was busy bathing my sisters. I was hatching a plot to relieve her candy dish of several orange slices staring me smack in the face. I couldn't believe it. A house full of people, and I was the only one in the front room. I leaned over the coffee table and smelled the aroma of the orange slices piercing my nose.

I slowly removed the metal top from the glass candy dish, the disk let out a loud pinging sound that went unheard because of all the noise coming from the kitchen, so I removed three orange slices from the dish, wrapped them in tissue and stuffed them deep in my pants pocket. Finally after three hours of waiting to take a bath I was called into the kitchen by my grandmother.

"Take off your clothes and get into the tub" she said, while standing by the stove boiling water.

The water was so hot I thought she was trying to boil lobster.

"Don't just look at the water" she said, "get in"

By the end of my bath I was exhausted, the hot water put me at ease, the bed was comfortable, in fact it was the softest bed I have ever slept on. Because I was the last one to take a bath and get in the bed I had to climb over my brothers and sisters and squeeze in the middle of the bed in a very dangerous spot. If the nocturnal monster showed his ugly face there will be no escaping that disaster.

By the time I made it to bed, my brothers and sisters had all fallen asleep, sleeping head to toe on a large queen size bed. This gave me ample opportunity to devour my ill-gotten gains. I laid in the bed nibbling away at my orange slices, listening to the 100-year-old house settled for the night. These were very uncertain times and even at a young age I detested not having control over my life. However the orange slice candy did provide a sense of comfort. I tried my best to stay awake, even holding my eyelids open up with my fingers, but the Sandman got the best of me. The next morning I was awoken by panic and screaming, my sister Tiana screamed bloody Hell.

"Mikey wet the bed!".

I was just as surprised as she was, I didn't know where or how the urine got their but nevertheless it was there. The nocturnal monster had paid me a visit, and I didn't even know where it came from or how to get rid of it. I just knew I was in trouble.

My grandfather was very irritated at the fact that I wet his bed and wanted to whip me with his razor strap; my grandfather was a tall, slim, fair skinned man with fine silk gray hair that displayed his Cherokee Indian heritage and his Irish roots. He was 6'3' tall, he stood towering over me with his razor strap in his right hand. I was afraid because I did not have my power ring, surprisingly my grandmother came to the rescue. She snatched the strap from him and told him to sit down. I was so ashamed and for once the brass spunky kid was nestling in a corner not wanting to show his face.

I was too embarrassed to sit at the kitchen table with everyone else so I sat in the front room and listened to the laughter echoing from the kitchen table and my sister Sherry praising the huge cornflake she found in her bowl of cereal. From this point on I was scared to death to fall asleep in their house. I tried my best not to drink water throughout the day, especially at night. This was a cardinal time in my Life. I was living in some-one's house other than my own home, with strange rules and traditional family meetings at the dinner table that didn't exist in my own home. I loved my grandparents, but I didn't know them, I felt disenfranchised and out of place.

My cousin Tommy lived with my grandparents and they treated him like royalty. He had carte blanche, he could go anywhere in the Ft 800.² house without limitations, including the cellar. He got to eat as much cake and candy as he wanted without anyone ques-tioning him. I was reduced to admiring the cake from a distance but somehow I was go-ing to have my way with that caramel cake sitting on the kitchen table freshly frosted. The cake didn't stand a chance as long as I was within a mile of it, my whole day was consumed with having a taste.

As usual after breakfast everyone ventured outside to play in the backyard. I patrolled around outside of the house, occasionally peaking in the kitchen at the caramel cake through the rusty screen fixed over the window on the side of house. My grandmother and aunt sat on the front porch having an idol conversation about church members and past buyers walking down the street. My siblings were preoccupied with my cousin, playing dodgeball in the backyard. This just gave me the perfect opportunity to creep into the house and relieve my grandmother's cake of some of its frosting.

I looked in all directions making sure the coast was clear, then I ran my finger along the bottom of the cake trying not to be detected. I scooped up about an inch of frosting. I couldn't believe it, I was successful just like the Joker on the Batman show. I thought to myself, staring at the inch of frosting smothering my finger, the Joker would be proud of me. Just as I was about to devour the evidence. A leather strap came flying out of no where and slapped me on my butt. I was so shocked I grabbed the seat of my pants smearing icing all of my pockets.

" Now get your butt outside" my grandfather said.

As he rolled the strap around his hand. I couldn't believe it, I almost got away with the perfect crime. After eating dinner that evening we all sat at the kitchen table and watched as my grandmother slice the caramel cake, placing it on wax paper and handing each of us a slice. Before she could give me a piece of cake my grandfather divulged our little secret.

"Mikey had enough cake for the night" he said.

"What do you mean by that"? My grandmother asked.

My grandfather looked at me out of the corner of his eye, he took a deep breath then walked out of the room. I set at the table with tears in my eyes, watching my sisters and brother pork down their caramel cake and chase it down with a tall glass of milk. Denton purposely demonstrated how good the cake taste, by savoring every bite, as he smiled at me, and chuckling to himself, then ran off into the backyard to chase lightning bugs. Everyone else finished their cake and adjourned to the front room to watch the Ed Sullivan show. I sat idle at the kitchen table in total disappointment. Just before my tears could hit the tablecloth, my grandmother slid a huge slice of caramel cake right under my nose, twice the size of my Brother's and sister's cakes, with a tall glass of refreshing milk to wash it all down.

I smiled as she rubbed her fingers in my curly hair, then adjourned to the front room. It took me twice the amount of time to eat my cake as it took the others. I rubbed my belly and smiled at Denton standing outside the kitchen door staring through the glass at my huge slice of cake. I was afraid to sit at the table much longer by myself, I could see the green dark spooky house next door from the kitchen window and it gave me the creeps. The Knox family lived next door to my grandmother. They were very elderly and seemed to be twice the age of my grandparents as if they had come from the 1850s during slavery.

Mr. Knox would walk down the street with his cane in hand, he seemed to be well over a hundred but at the same time he was ambulatory. I waited till he got near the edge of the fence, then I ran from behind the bushes and barked as though I was a large dog. He playfully turned to me and said.

"I'm going to cut your ear off."

Tiana and I loved trying to scare Mr. Knox. It wasn't until the week before our departure that we discovered he was our great-grandfather on our father's side of the family. All of a sudden I was no longer scared of him or his wife or their dark house. I even made it my business to go over and have a casual conversation with them on their front porch. I wasn't emotionally connected to them, it was just nice to see the other side of my family.

$\mathcal{H}$illside st

Martindale-Brightwood is a neighborhood situated on the near northeast side of Indianapolis bounded by 30th Street, Massachusetts Avenue, 21st Street, Sherman Drive, and the North folk Southern Railroad tracks. This area encompasses two previously independent settlements.

After my mother was back on her feet we moved into our own two bed room house located on Hillside Street. The house had a chicken coop, a barn, and a garage. The new addition to the family had arrived which meant I could push someone around. Before Denise was three she and my brother Denton went to live with my grandparents. Tiana became my best friend until she started school the following year in 1963. I was left alone with my mother and her boyfriend Andy.

Andy was not a handsome man, in fact he look like he was fresh off the boat from Africa, but he was a hard worker, a "Hustler". I believe that's what my mother liked about him. I found them both extremely boring to spend my day with. I rode in the backseat of his pink 1950 Buick while he handed me a large half eaten France's big boy hamburger. The sandwich was too big for me to fit in my mouth but it tasted delicious as I nibble around the edges.

I enjoyed that hamburger but I had things I wanted to do, such as climb on the garage and walk on the railroad tracks or play inside the big empty abandoned school with rotting floorboards that sat on top of the hill behind our house. It was once believed that John Dillinger and his gang used the school for their hideout. Other than spending time with my mother and her boyfriend, I spent small periods of my time with my dog Frisky. Playing in the backyard until we were both were exhausted, we leaned against the back of the house, I rubbed her belly while eating a grocery bag size full of green apples. I ate until I was blue in the face, apple after apple.

Spending the entire morning with my mother made the day long and boring. I would find myself gazing out the window at the end of the block, hoping Tiana would soon turn the corner. She was my best friend and I could not wait to see her and here tales of her day in school. Tiana and I would spend most of our time fighting one another or making mud pies, either way we were happy just playing together. She was the bigger kid and a little crazy so I did all I could to avoid fighting with her. Tiana had a violent temper, she would often get mad and throw uncontrollable fits if things didn't go her way.

Summertime had arrived once again which meant Denton was packing his bags and heading back home. We played together well as long as I did what he said and stayed away from him and his friends. Denton and his friends were very creative when it came to finding things to do. They pushed a large truck tire to the top of the hill. Once they stopped, they began whispering to one another, all the sudden they looked in my direction.

"Climb in" Denton said.

Once I climbed inside the tire, he shoved the tire down the steep hill right into the cross traffic. A car came to a screeching halt but not before slamming into the tire knocking me a block and a half down the street. Denton laughed as he picked the tire up.

" You'll be okay, don't go home crying to mama's like a baby" he said.

While rolling the tire back up the hill. " You wanted to hang with the big boys remember". I made no bones about it, I Just followed him back uphill.

The police arrived just as we reached the top of the hill getting ready for another run. We dropped the tires then ran in different directions. I was the smallest, but I wasn't the slowest. Buggy was three years older than I but he was as big as a house and couldn't keep up with the rest of the group, so he just hid in the garage.

Once the police officers were out of view we thought it will be fun to climb on the stack of old tires along side of the garage window. We invented another game called paratroopers, climbing up the tires and onto the garage, then jumping off the garage onto the stack of tires. Buggy was as slow as molasses. I could climb up on the garage, jump down, then climb back up before he could jump off the garage. I grew very impatient with his morbidly obese body. He stood at the edge of the garage teetering, trying to build up courage to jump. I couldn't take anymore, so I shoved him off the garage head first onto the tires. He slowly dragged himself from the tires holding his side, crying as if he had been hit by a freight train. Instantly he was enraged. "I'm going to kill you" holding his side chasing me around the yard. He tried to catch me but I was just too fast. I eventually ran into the house leaving him by the garage in tears.

The day turned into night, allowing the crickets to make music and the lightning bugs to beautify the night with their yellow lights. I could hear rocks bouncing off the side of the house." Oh boy I thought, a rock Battle". I sprang to my feet and ran right in the middle of the battle. I didn't care which side I was on, so I began throwing rocks in both directions. I didn't care who I hit or if I got hit, I just wanted to throw rocks. I wasn't good at hiding but I was good at throwing. I stuck my head around the corner to peek at my aggressors, within seconds a huge rock busted me right in the middle of my forehead. I hit the ground like a sack of potatoes, dust flying in the air as I laid on the ground lifelessly.

"I think your brother was hurt, Denton" Buddy said.

As he chuckled to himself.

"That's what you get punk for pushing me off the garage".

The rock battle stopped mid stream to allow my brother to drag me into the house. Once again I lay in the hospital with my mother sitting beside the bed waiting for me to wake up. Two weeks later I was back outside, full steam ahead, playing freeze tag in the backyard. It was getting late in the hour around 8 o'clock at night. It was so dark along the grass cover path between our houses I couldn't see my hands in front my face. Buggy jumped from the bushes scaring me half to death, I took off running like a bat out of hell, all of a sudden I tripped and fell face down on a large brick. I didn't feel any pain, so I didn't think anything was wrong. I got up and staggered my way into the house. Tiana looked up and started yelling.

"Mikey got blood all over his face".

My mother came running from the bathroom,

" Boy you need stitches again, call Dorothy to see if she can give me a ride to the hospital".

Within two weeks time I was a bloody mess, two accidents in two weeks. My mother thought I was accident prone, and she do not buy a house near a river because she knew it would be too much temptation for me to handle.

Another year went by and I still was denied entrance in the public school. Since my birthday was in December I was forced to wait until the following year. Life wasn't all bad, after school Tiana and I picked green apples from the tree behind our garage. We'd spend hours picking bags of apples. Tiana stopped eating when she got full, I kept eating until all the apples were gone, pouring salt on top of the apples with every bite. Within three hours of eating all the green apples I begin choking on my tongue, my mother wasn't even a nurse yet but she knew what to do. She put a spoon down my throat to hold my tongue in place, allowing me to breath while transporting me to the hospital. I was put to sleep while my stomach was being pumped. I awakened to black Charcoal residue around my mouth.

" Damn, I have to keep my eye on you every second" my mother said.

After the last incident she appointed my older sister 'Sherry' as my personal babysitter. I I didn't recognize her authority and never listened to anything she said. She was a pushover. Tiana and I ran around the house like wild heathens, eating all the peanut butter and jelly we could find. Sherry did her best to control us, we only quieted down when she threatened to tell our mother of our unruly and mischievous behavior. The only time I was quiet was when Tiana was in school. The rest of the day we were both hell raisers.

Tiana went to school everyday leaving a huge blank spot in my day. I was always in search of something to do. I was quickly out growing riding around in the backseat of Andy's car. I needed to be in school and Tiana wasted no time telling me the horror stories about kindergarten and how scary school was. She even pointed out how big the needles were that went into our arm because every student was required to get a vaccination shot. Tiana had always been an agitator and she was proving it to the last minute. The fall has once again emerged for the fourth time in my young life. Colorful leaves lie lifelessly on the ground. Trick-or-treaters kick their way through the piles of leaves stacked in the front yard. Turkeys roasting in the oven for Thanksgiving and Christmas was just a blink of an eye away. For the first time in my life I was made to feel special on December 4. Andy called me into the bedroom, he lit four candles and had me practice blowing them out. He escorted me to the kitchen table where a large cake with my name printed right in the middle. 'Happy birthday Mikey'.

I felt so loved I almost cried. I blew the candles out and rip the box away from around my Long ranger cowboy pistols. He even gave me a horse. A horse head on a stick, that I rolled around in circles kicking up dust driving my siblings crazy. Denting got so mad he grabbed the horse and tossed it into the Street into the oncoming traffic. I didn't even break stride or look in any direction as I ran head first into the street chasing down my horse. Cars and trucks came to a screeching halt smoke coming from the wheels. My mother and siblings screaming from the front porch as I stood stand-fast in traffic wiping the dirt from my horse. I took my time mounting my heart in the street, then off into the sunset I rode. My birthday was just a tidbit If what Christmas would be like.

This Christmas would it be much different then any other Christmas I've ever had. With my father nesting in prison, Andy took full charge of the household. He purchase two sets of bunk beds stacked three high, he pay the bills and purchased food. I thought he was a nice guy but it was all put into perspective the night he and my mother were entertaining guests. I was summonsed to go into the bedroom to get an ashtray. I was only four years old, a typical kid. Once I stepped into the bedroom and saw all those toys stacked on the bed, every square foot of the bed covered from the foot of the bed to the headboard, up to the ceiling. It was as if I had just walked into a toy factory. I couldn't help but to examine them and before I knew it 10 minutes had gone by. Andy stepped in the bathroom,

" Were you playing with these toys boy?" Andy said.
 No, I said, I'm just trying to find an ashtray"

I stood there with a cap gun in my hand trying to explain myself. But Andy wasn't buying my excuse. He pulled the belt from around his waist, grabbing my right arm he swung his belt. I jumped in the air and he missed. I had his rhythm down perfect, every time he swung the belt I jumped in the air causing him to miss. But all of a sudden he got smart, he pretended as though he was going to swing the belt, I jumped, he waited for me to land on the ground then swatted me with the belt. I ran into the bedroom and climbed over the railing of my baby bed. I was four years old still sleeping in an infants crib because my sisters feared the nocturnal monster. Each morning my sister Marcia lift me from the bed and placed me on the floor. Everyone has their own bed except for me. I slept where I can fit in. Every few months prior I was sleeping with my mother in her bed but once Andy moved into the house I was hastily exported to my siblings bedroom.

My days were long I mentally exhausting, because I was a four-year-old nothing to do. However; my turn did come for attending school and I was going to make sure that my mother was going to be there each and every day with me. I never been away from my mother for more than a week at a time but if I was away from her more than a week at a time I had my grandparents as a support system in her absence.

I gladly walked to school with my mother and siblings. My mother gladly escorted me to my kindergarten class and set attentively by the teacher's desk (Mrs. Collie). The classroom was filled with children that appeared to be my age. Most of the children seem to have been groomed for the first day of school, they played idly at their small round tables and appeared to be having fun. The atmosphere seemed pleasant and I couldn't wait to get started.

I sat on the floor in front of Ms. Collie's desk drawing on a blank piece of paper she handed me. As she talked to my mother, I neatly removed one crayon at a time from the box and systematically replaced it when I was done using the Crayon. Occasionally I'd stopped drawing and gazed in my mother's direction trying to get a glimpse of her. Each time I looked up my mother had moved to a different part of the room seemingly closer to the door, then eventually out of the classroom.

It was my first time being away from her, and I fell instantly to pieces, kicking, screaming, and ripping the paper in half and throwing crayons across the room, the teacher's desk was the biggest target within reach and I wasted no time in expressing my artistic ability. I hastily drew pictures on the desk, mostly scribbling unrecognizable lines as though I was a great artist, one step from cutting my ear off. I heard a little girl say.

" Look at him Mrs. Collie, he's drawing on your desk".

Not bound by any corporal punishment laws Ms. Collie snatched me up by the rear of my pants, slapping me so hard on my butt I thought I was shot, then scorned me for acting like a three-year-old. She ripped a large brown piece of paper from the roller hanging from the wall, tossing it on the floor in front of her desk and forced me to set in the middle of the paper, once Ms. Collie walked back towards her desk, I violently shoved the paper from under my legs and began drawing on the floor.

Ms. Collie became outraged. She exploded out of her chair, snatched me from the floor and hastily escorted me to the corner of the room where I stood for more than an hour facing the wall until it was time to take a nap.

This type of discipline was new to me. I couldn't understand why I obeyed her the first time she punished me, normally it would take me six or seven times before I got the message. Mrs. Collie ordered me to retrieve my sleeping pad from the corner and lie down. I slumped sedately toward the ground managing to avoid hitting my well bruised fanny on the linoleum floor. My first year in school went moving by fast, I soon discover-Tiana was telling the truth about getting shots and the endless stack of needles located on a cart to the right of the entryway. Everyone did get shots, the line stretched around the corner and down the steps. We were all lined up outside the nurses office, one kid more scared than the other. I could here kids screaming and crying, then walking out of the nurse's office holding their arm weeping with a little speck of blood showing on the bandage. The closer I got to the door the more anxious I got.

The line shrinked one person at a time, and finally I was next in line to go in the nurse office. The nurse stepped outside the door wearing white shoes, white hat and white dress. She reminded me of the ushers at my grandmother's church. She stood over me looking down, grinning like a cheshire cat on Alice in Wonderland. Her huge white hand reached out to grab my arm. The back of her hand was so hairy I thought I was being grabbed by a grizzly bear, so I took off running down the hallway.

" Catch him!" she yelled.

As I scurried down the hallway and up the double wide stair case. No one could catch me, I was running for my life. I was so fast, my sister Marica was brought from her classroom to the nurse's office to help catch me. She told me to calm down as she stood by the nurse's office blocking the door to ensure that I got my shots. I hesitantly walked inside the nurse's office. The walls were lined with white wood and glass cabinets, there was a metal cart full of syringes and the room smelled of alcohol, a familiar stench I recognized from my past visits to the hospitals.

I was in familiar surroundings, but this time the needles were a little longer. Cotton balls and several bottles of a clear solution were lined up on the table. The nurse raised the needle high in the air and shoved it into the bottle of clear solution. "This is not going to hurt, your just going to feel a little pinch" she said, then wiped my arm with a wet cotton ball. I yelled and screamed bloody hell.

" It's just a cotton ball little boy, see it's just a cotton ball".

The nurse said. I calmed down for a split second right before she shoved the 12 inch needle in my arm.

$\mathcal{A}$ marriage of convenience

Time passed and I adjusted to school life well. I no longer missed my mother's presence or longed for the long boring rides in the back of Andy's car. I was under a new environment, a new system that measured and challenged my behaviors, whether they were positive or negative. The school system taught me, for every action there is a reaction. The year had passed, I was now in the first grade, the kids where more advanced in reading, math and social skills. I seem to have been doing okay, not like Tiana, who repeated kindergarten due to her outlandish behavior. I passed kindergarten the first time around and happily took my place amongst my fellow kindergarten graduates in the first grade.

My social skills were soon put to the test when a love letter was passed to me by one of the prettiest girls in the class. I was so shocked that she noticed me, I sat there with the unfolded letter in my hand. Took a deep breath and slowly slid it on the desk and quietly unfolded the letter as it clung to my sweaty palms. In the letter, she asked if I would marry Stella Glass and she would marry the another boy in the class. I hastily replied. "I want to marry you, let him marry Stellar Glass". I folded the letter, then scanned the classroom for the whereabouts of my teacher. I leaned forward to pass the note back to the pretty girl.

As luck would have it, my teacher was in my blind spot and before I knew it the teacher was quick to grab my hand pulling me to the front of the classroom, holding my arm high in the air displaying the letter for the entire class to see. She called the other three note passers to the front of the class, then marched all of us to the principal's office. We sat in the hallway awaiting for our day of execution.

The principal's office was the forbidden zone; because anytime you were summoned to such a high office it would mean you would have to face the (Pedal), a long wooden board used to discipline students by giving them three whacks on their bottoms if they became disruptive. The heavy wooden door to the principal's office opened, I could barely move as I stared at the 250 lb. men who occupy the entire space of the doorway.

He lined us up in front of his desk, after looking us over; he reached over to his book-shelf and removed a big black book. The words were to advanced for me to compre-hend. I recognize the book, it was the same book my grandmother Carrie to church every Sunday.

(The principal) "Stella Glass lock arms together with Michael and you other two kids do the same".

He began reading from the book which he had pulled from his shelf, I didn't understand what he was doing or the reason that he was reading out of that book. Stella was smil-ing as if she understood every word the principle was saying.   It all came together when he said.
 "I now pronounce you man and wife".

Blood rushed to my head, tears began streaming down my face. Stella grabbed my arm smiling while lying her head on my shoulder keeping me from breaking free of our pseudo bond.

Here I was married to the most unattractive girl, not just in the class but in the entire school, her bifocal glasses and her uncombed hair threw me into a frantic plea for my freedom.

(Mikey) "I promised to never pass another note as long as I live if you would release me from this marriage".

The principle and the teacher could barely contain themselves from laughing out loud, he held the book in front of his face and the teacher turned towards the wall to muffle her mouth with her hand to keep from laughing out loud.

The principal agreed to annul this marriage as long as we all agreed not to pass any more notes in school. This was a lesson I would never forget, I can't remember the last time I passed a note in or out of school. The day passed fast, it was a Friday and life was good, I was free of wife and single again.

Once that school bell sounded I was off to the Christian center were the fun began. Just as I entered the door my sister Sherry pulled me to the side and whispered in my ear.

"Daddy's home from prison".

I dropped my creative basket and ran for home as though I had won a candy raffle. My mother and Andy were standing on the sidewalk. Andy handed her something then walked away. I was so excited I bounced onto the front porch as if I was on the spring-board, just as I stretched my hand for the door knob, my mother grabbed my wrist and said "wait a minute Mikey".

She pushed the door all the way open, something was obstructing the door from opening completely.

(Mom) "Come from behind the door Raymond".

My father stepped from behind the door with a knife in his hand,(father) "I'm going to cut you up". I stood there waiting for my mother to run. Had she ran I wouldn't have been far behind her, but she didn't run. She stood her ground, she invited him to come forward with his knife and he obliged her. He came toward her knife in hand, I felt powerless, and I thought surely she was going to die.

Once he got within 12 feet she pulled a small gun from her trench coat and dropped it down to her side. He stopped dead in his tracks.

(Mom) "What did you say you were going to do 'mother Fucker?"

(Father) "Wait a minute Phyllis".

She fired once at his feet, he jumped and moved closer, she shot the gun two more times at his feet then yelled.

"Dance motherfucker". The next shoot was in his leg.

(Father yelling) "Phyllis, Phyllis, Phyllis"!

As he fell to the floor with both hands clutching his leg, blood pouring between his fingers and onto his London fall trench coat, he begged her not to shoot him again. I backed into a corner watching from a distance as the drama unfolded. Once again the police had come to our house, and once again my father was returned to prison to complete his prison time for violating his parole.

Now I was truly a displaced child in a dysfunctional home torn between the love for my two parents. I feared for the life of my father, and the safety of my mother. The police arrived before my father could walk away, they handcuffed him as I watched them escort him into an ambulance and drive away. Once again I stared at my father leaving with my face pressed against the front room window. Tears pierced my eyes and flowed freely down my badly worn winter coat. I could since It would be a long time before I would see or hear from him again.

These were confusing and frustrating times. I wanted nothing more than to escape this roller coaster ride of emotion and uncertainty. Months sailed by and I hadn't hear from my father sense he had gone back to prison for attempted assault with a deadly weapon. Andy departed and he took his new bunkbeds with him. I guess I could say I don't blame him. He didn't want to put up with the baby daddy drama. The Christmas of 1965 would be the harshest Christmas, so I thought. We had nothing in the house that resemble the holiday spirit. Fortunate for my mother someone new about her dilemma, they were courteous enough to place her name in a basket at someone's church. I was young but I could feel the emptiness in the house, the absence of Andy's spirit, especially his spirit of giving. There was a knock at the door, and I did exactly as I was instructed not to do.

I opened the door and allow three strangers to walk in our house. One white male and two white females entered the room. They said they were from a church and they were given I name to sponsor for Christmas. They dragged in a huge Christmas tree, the tree was so tall it scraped the ceiling and had to be taken back outside and cut to the correct size. We pop popcorn, made ornaments and put it on thread and wrapped it around the Christmas tree. We sang Christmas carols, and baked cookies and prepared a Christmas dinner fit or a King. They gave us plastic toy blocks as Christmas gifts, and dolls for my sisters. It wasn't anything expensive or extravagant but somehow the Christmas spirit was upon us and we were happier then we ever have been doing this holiday season.

My mother had moved onto a new life and a new relationship. She try her hand at the prospect of dating someone from another race. Too young well-dressed white man appeared at our front door, looking dapper, wearing white dress shirts, ties and trench coats. One of the young man came bearing ice cream cones for all of us. It wasn't meant for the young white gentleman to see us. My auntie thought it best that she bring them over to meet my mothers children, seeing how she only had one child. I guess she wanted to discourage the young man from dating my mother and it worked, we never saw them again. I guess the thought of dating a woman with seven kids was too much for him so he opted out. However, I must say he delivers swell ice cream.

Rayford was still running around the streets at 10 years old and I was still the only male member of my family consistently at home during sleeping hours. Rayford spent a lot of time chasing women even at a very young age he stayed out until the waking hours of the next morning. I thought my big brother could beat anyone and wasn't afraid of anything, little did I know he was afraid of a bully that lived several blocks from us. The bully was a young kid that had family problems. He decided to act out his dysfunctional family ways on his friends and anyone within reach. Unfortunate for my brother he was chosen by this kid to act out his frustrations. My brother didn't want to fight and just walked away but the kid push the envelope forcing the fight. Finally he crossed the line grabbing my brother by the arm ripping his shirt. Rayford lit into him like a match to gasoline. He returned home later that afternoon looking as though he just been through a tornado, buttons were ripped off his shirt, blood dripping slightly from his nose. He gave it is good as he got and discovered the boy wasn't as tough as he thought he was, as a matter of fact he won the fight very easily. The boy never bothered Rayford again, the bully maintained his distance the remainder of the year.

𝒟elaware Street- out of sight, out of mind

A few months later, into my life walks Bryce 5ft '5' inches tall and 157lbs, slanted eyes as though he was of the Chinese descent. His temperament was hard to grasp. I stayed away from him as much as possible because I knew if anything were to happen between us it would be good. Spring was forging straight ahead pushing flowers out of the ground for our appreciation, filling the air with frequently fresh scents for the new year. Snow was slow to melt and remanence of slush line the sewers waiting for their final farewell and hello to the 50° weather welcoming spring time.

The closer summer got the more I noticed boxes stacked in corners throughout the house. Easter was here and my sisters begin preparing for a traditional trip to our grandmother's church. The Saturday before Easter we paid a visit to my auntie Dorothy's house, a small two bedroom house on the West side of town. My sister wanted her ears pierced, but there was no extra money around the house for such luxury items. Marica always admired Dorothy's earrings, and was fascinated by the fact the Dorothy Pierced her owners ears. Marcia ask my mother if it was okay to allow Dorothy to piercing her ears. "They're your ears" my mother said. Dorothy agreed and before 12 noon we are on our way to her house.

I loved visiting my aunties house. She always had a coffee cake sitting on the kitchen table and her house always smelled fresh and clean. The only annoyance wasn't two ankle biting dogs that seemed to never shut up. My uncle George was always in the garage pretending like he was fixing his cars but his real reason for being in the garage was to have a couple of beers without his wife's interference.

The ear piercing process began. Dorothy removed a needle from her sewing kit and placed it on the stove burner. Marcia's eyes grew big with fright as the needle turned burning hot red. I sat at the kitchen table waiting for the incident to unfold, but occasionally I was distracted by the coffee cake sitting on the kitchen counter. My auntie removed a block of ice from the refrigerator, wrapped it in a towel and sat it on the table next to my sister. "Bend your head to the side" she said, while removing the red hot needle from the stove. I couldn't help but laugh, while Marcia sat at the table tapping her feet frantically. As the needle got close to her ear she began to lose all control.

As the sizzling red hot needle passed her eyes, she screamed.

"Wait!".

"What's wrong". Dorothy said.

(Marcia) "You're not going to put that in my ear are you?"

"No silly, I have to cool it off with ice, but I had to sterilize it with the fire". Dorothy said.

I began laughing so hard Dorothy gave me a piece of coffee cake just to shut my mouth. She stuck the needle through Marcia's ears with a piece of thread on the end.

"Hand me those scissors Mikey"

I picked up the scissors and handed them to her point first. Dorothy screamed and yelled.

"Turn them around! Turn them around and hand me the other end".

I didn't know what all the drama was about but I did as she requested. I turned the scissors around and handed them to her with the point facing me. Tiana was next in line to have her ears pierced, or should I say roasted like two marshmallows. Marcia cried her way into the front room holding toilet paper to her ears. Tiana followed Marcia into the front room not wanting any part of Dorothy's homemade stove top ear piercing, done for free method. Tiana rushed into the front room, eyes bugging out of her head.

"Okay Tiana, it's your turn." Dorothy said.

While sterilizing two needles on the kitchen stove. Tiana ran onto the front porch ignoring Dorothy's requests to come to the kitchen.

"I'll get my ears pierced next time" Tiana said.Shaking her head no.

Dorothy was extremely disappointed she didn't get to Pierce Tiana's ears. I ventured into the back yard to talk to my uncle George and laughed as he secretly removed beers from the small refrigerator in his garage. My auntie loves her husband and didn't want him to drink, jeopardizing his health but he was bound to have a beer unknown by his wife.

I got a kick out of being around the odd couple. Dorothy was a very light, fair skinned woman. She beautifully resembled Lena Horne. She was a high strung, hypochondriac, who loved her husband so much she thought other women crave him as well. George was a 5 foot five, slightly overweight man, with buckeyes. He often moved at a turtle's pace, wearing a fisherman's hat and deck shoes as though he were going onto a boat. I didn't spend much time at their house because there was nothing to do other then play with their dogs or sit idly by and watch my uncle work on his car. If we stayed long enough we were forced to hear Dorothy's rendition of some up notches 1950s song on her newly purchased organ. For its time, the organ was very elaborate. Having several buttons that could alter sound and create different musical instruments.

I sat slumped on her couch saturated with plastic covering slowly dehydrating as she belted it out lyrics to a song I did not understand. Then came the church music and out door I went, running down the street as though I was running from a haunted house. I Stopped by Mr. Sneed's candy store grabbed two packs of Now and Later's, then hopped onto my grandmothers porch, where I sat rocking back and forth in her red metal non-rocking chairs. I slid two Now & Laters into my mouth before barely getting them out of the wrapper. The juices from the banana and grape Now & Laters flowed freely as I watched lightning bugs light up the front yard by the thousands, bumblebees settled in for the night inside of huge some flowers tucked in the far reaches of the corner of the yard held up by a wire attached to the fence pole. Worms dug their way deep into the ground hiding under my grandmother's tomato patch, trying to escape the hands of feisty kids and fishermen waiting for the sun to rise.

For once in my life I had a moment of silence, looking over the tall vegetable garden that slightly blocked my view of the church across the street. I wonder about my life, and where I would be 10 years from this time. I wonder who would still be in my life 10 years from now and what role would they play. This was my mental quiet place, a place that I went all by myself. The aroma of freshly cooked greens and ham sitting on the stove. A vanilla cake smothered with chocolate icing. A candy dish full of candy that no one was allowed to touch, five red chairs lined up on the front porch, a backyard with a functioning water pump from the 1940s era and a metal tub hanging on the outside of the house displaying the changing world.

Ever Easter Sunday like clock work we went to church escorted by our grandmother. I didn't mind attending church once a year only if I went with my grandmother. I knew right after church I could look forward to playing at her backyard and ending our day with a piece of cake wrapped in wax paper. The church was hot, with an antiquated cooling system. Nonfunctioning swamp coolers sat in the windows, the only fans the church had were the hand fans donated by the local funeral parlor. The first two rows were filled with old men appearing to be near death. The entire congregation appeared to have been born in the 1800s.

The preacher screamed a incomprehensible from the pool pit of fire and brimstone as he waved his handkerchief in the air. The old women waved back praised God as I slept into heat exhaustion. My freshly pressed green suit jacket fail to the floor. The wooden pews were just about getting the best of me, so I threw my hand in the air requesting a bathroom break. Tiana and I had the same idea and we stood outside long enough to get a breath of fresh air. Just as we were having fun running around outside the church, one of the ushers grabbed us by the shirt escorting us back to our seat.

" One more hour and this nightmare will be over with".

I thought to myself, flipping my .20 cent around in the palm of my hand with visions of great Now & Laters dancing in my head.Once I was released from church I ran straight to Mr. Sneeze's Candy store and purchased four packs of Now & Laters.

The temperature heat it up all across the sleepy town over the course of the next two months. After a long frostbitten winter the summer Crept its way in. the sun shone brilliantly through my window. The summer had arrived, and once again in my peripatetic childhood we move into a really quiet secluded neighborhood on 30th & Delaware Street. The neighborhood was much different from our prior address and the house was three times the size. It was a three bedroom house with an attic and a basement. Toys were scattered throughout the attic and in the toy box in the living room. It was as if the prior renters knew I was coming. A pair of pearl white ice skates caught my attention. I quickly put them on and ran up and down the street trying to skate. "Those are for ice you idiot" said the boy next door. "I know what therefore, just leave me alone". I said taking off the skates and running in the house. Sam finally met my mother's request, he placed us in a nice home, in a nice neighborhood. After all these years he still managed to be our landlord.

The neighborhood was composed of a mixed race of people, meaning there were both black and white people who lived on this street. The long drawn out civil rights movement was at its height, and European Americans were moving out of the inner-city and into the suburbs away from the onslaught of blacks moving into the inner-city.

Although most of the white people were retired, or over sixty years old, the African Americans were young vigorous people in their early 30s. The neighborhood was quiet and clean, most of the homes had three stories, either with a basement or an attic. Sometimes the homes had a basement and an attic and a two car garage. The Blocks were long and wide and seem to disappear at the top of the hill. I didn't haste to cruse the new neighborhood looking at the big homes with large front porches and huge back yards.

I was even capable of making a couple of friends directly across the street from my house. Frankie, Joe and I became friends immediately. There was also a cute little girl that lived next door, she was at least a year younger than I. Her brother detested the fact Lisa and I spent so much time together, I was only seven years old and Lisa was only 5 1/2 but for some strange reason he felt we were doing more than just making mud pies. Every time we played in the backyard he would encroach on our fun.

"Go home, you're too old to play with her" he said.

Shoving me toward the back fence.

"Don't touch me again" I said.

While standing my ground. He pushed me one more time, I had an immediate reaction. I grabbed a switch from the boysenberry tree then slapped him across the face with it.

"Oh shit" he said, clutching his face.

Tears formed in his eyes, He was 13 years old and a much bigger kid then I. He outweighed me by 60 pounds. He would have no trouble throwing me around the yard if he chose to, but he decided to punch me in the nose then shove me out of his yard. My nose began bleeding profusely as I searched the ground for a rock to strike him with. Before long my "white buddy El" tennis shoes were covered with blood. I was so pre-oc-cupied with my tennis shoes being ruined by the bloodstains. I rushed upstairs to the bathroom and soaked them in the bathtub in ice cold water before the blood could set in. Over the course of time he came to realize I would continue to play with his sister, and I came to realize making mud pies wasn't worth getting a bloody nose every week, so I spent my free time across the street at Joe's and Frank's house.

.

Moving to a new location was always fun, but there was one small problem, Bryce fol-lowed us into our new home and adopted a lotus-eater life style, because he didn't have the discipline to reconciled his income with his bills. He never spoke or said anything to me until that fateful hour late one evening.

I was sitting idly gazing out my bedroom window when approached by Rayford carrying an unopened bar of soap he just purchased from the variety store earlier in the day. He cut the box away from the soap using a small carving knife, with his artistic ability he was able to carve his initials very artistically into the soap. He handed me the bar of soap and asked if I would like to do the same. Smelling from ear to ear, I was glad to oblige him. I began carving my initials in large letters. Rayford said. "Wow! let me see that man, it's really good I'm going to go show mama". Rayford grabbed the soap and ran downstairs like his pants on were on fire.

I don't believe it, he tricked me, now mom is going to yell and scream at me. But that wasn't the case. Bryce had to prove he was the head of the house. I turned around and there I saw a silhouette of his 5 foot tall frame in the door eclipsing the light entering the bedroom from the hallway. He stood there posturing with his machismo attitude. He was short in stature but his muscular frame took up the entire structure of the door. (Bryce) "take them off" (Mikey) "take what off"? (Bryce) "your pants and underwear". I thought to myself. " this fool must be crazy".

I froze like a mannequin in a Macy's window. I didn't know what to do or make of what I thought I heard or whether I understood him. He repeated it again, (Bryce) "take off all of your clothes, you're going to get a whipping for playing with and wasting soap. I couldn't believe it, this man must have lost his mind, he's going to beat me with that razor strap for such a small infraction. I hesitantly drop my pants down to my ankles, (Bryce), take everything off including your underwear.

I began shaking uncontrollably like leaves on a tree as I braced myself, he lifted his razor strap high in the air scraping the light fixture on the ceiling. He blazingly swung the big leather strap, hitting the back of my legs and my butt, cutting deeply into my flesh as though I was a runaway slave. Once the beating begin my brother Rayford sat in the kitchen clutching the kitchen table, realizing he made a mistake as I screamed bloody hell while the razor strap dug deep into my seven-year-old virgin Flesh, leaving three-inch web marks across my back, legs and my butt. I fell on the bed shaking and crying in disbelief. I collapsed on the bed and cried myself into a twilight sleep.

I didn't know what just happened but if this was what my life was going to be like until my mother dumped this idiot, I wasn't going to stick around for maltreatment and getting beat half to death for minor infractions. I took my sister's scarf and placed my best T-shirt and a clean pair of underwear in the scarf, tied it around a stick and off I went down the street. My sisters stood in the doorway crying, my mother said let him go he'll be back. I was determined to be on my own. I knew I could cut grass in the summer and shovel snow in winter and I will be okay.

I walked briskly down the street to my friend Peanut's apartment building where I stayed for two hours playing football on an electric football board. I sat passively and allowed Peanut's to cheat. Every time his players carried the ball, Peanuts turned the vibration up on the football machine just enough so that his players could sail smoothly across the football field. But once it was my team turn to carry the football, he would turned the machine up really high so that my players will fall over on the football field allowing him to retrieve the ball. I stayed and played as long as I could, until it was time for them to eat dinner.

Their mother asked that I come back after they finished eating their dinner. I walked slowly to the door looking back over my shoulders waiting for in invitation to stay for dinner. I can't help to wonder why she didn't invited me to stay for dinner, so I walked up and down the hallway for 35 minutes until they were done eating dinner then back to the football board where peanut cheated his way to another victory. Sooner or later the overwhelming smell of leftover meatloaf, mashed potatoes and gravy became too much. I found myself subliminally walking out of the apartment and down the stairs to the dim lit streets.

I can see my little gray house resting quietly in the middle of the block but I was determined not to go home. 8 o'clock was approaching fast, I knew I had to be somewhere, part of my social recognition training said that when the street lights flickered on, I had to be in front of the house and once the lights were totally on, I had to be in the house. Somehow this training stayed with me. So I stared down 30th St. and Talbot where the bully live.

I knew that leaving wasn't an option, so I headed back towards my home just in time for my mother to step out on the front porch and yeah.

"Boy get in this house".

I reluctantly sashayed into the living room then escorted to the kitchen table for large bowl of Lima beans and one squarely cut slice of unsweetened cornbread. I hated Lima beans I would rather starve than eat those big half cooked, hard to swallow horse pills. I sat at the kitchen table never touching the beans and fell asleep in the chair. I awakened to find myself tucked securely in my bed. It was always a battle when we had black-eyed peas or Lima beans. My sister Tiana was the driving force causing me to rebel against eating Lima beans. She quite the agitator, she didn't help the situation any, she always told me that black-eyed peas were eyes of dead people and they stared at me while I tried to eat them from the bowl. I was horrified at the thought, and wouldn't go within 10 feet of a bowl of black-eyed peas. She often played pranks on me and threatened to beat me up if I didn't comply to her wishes. Tiana was a rapscallion everywhere she went she brought disarray with her.

Within the last three months my mother seemed very rushed. I didn't understand why until I discovered she was in nursing school and I couldn't have been more proud of her, because she was working and attending school as the same time. We were on welfare, receiving food stamps for the time being while she was in night school. The welfare system didn't allow her to go to school and receive general assistance. Fortunately one of the welfare supervisor recognized the potential in my mother and she allowed her to attended college and work to support her seven children while receiving a small amount of food stamps. I watched my mother leave early in the mornings and return late at night. She would fix our lunch for the next day of school and place it in the refrigerator.

She ironed our clothes and laid them neatly on the couch. She would stack quarters, dimes and nickels on the kitchen counter for my elder brothers and sisters bus fare and lunch. This was just part of her daily routine, her face carried a scorned expression. I sat quietly on her bed and watched as she pressed out a stack of freshly dried clothes, sprinkling water from a loosely capped bottle of water over the clothes as she pressed and squeezed the wrinkles out of our pants.

It was that time of year again: the bitter wet and cold weather that challenged her character as she treads through the snow, books in hand, walking down the middle of the unsnow plowed streets. I watched her until she turned the corner or I could not see her any more, this became routine for me and I never missed a beat. For the next 9 months I would run to the front bedroom to watch her leave for school, and then I would run down stairs to put on a freshly ironed shirt and pair of pants hurrying to get dressed for school. Every morning I would venture across the street to Frank's house so that we could walk to school together. His mother thought I had beautiful hair, but I needed to comb it. She slowly approached me with a comb behind her back.

" You have such pretty hair, can I comb your hair?" she said.

As she raised the comb in the air. I violently shook my head no as I ran and ducked under their kitchen table. Every morning it was the same thing, she wanted to comb my hair and I retreated under the kitchen table.

School #60 William Bell was an antiquated school as if it was a throwback from the 1940s construction error. Little to no remolding had been done to the school, the bathroom urinals stretched down to the floor and a large metal fountain with a floor paddle that we press to wash our hands encompassed most of the bathroom. The main entrance into the school was a big double door with one single door on each end of the building. The school was a hand-me-down from the middle class white's that moved out of the neighborhood, who left the school district for suburban living and leaving the school in need of much repair. The old black chalkboards and the lift top desk were outdated, so was the public school systems policies on corporal punishment. A long wooden paddle was the only form of discipline and if the principal got creative he would drill holes in the paddle to increase the speed of the swing and provide suction on impact.

The head principal was named Mr. Lackey, a short 5 foot tall 350 pound man with at least a 54 inch waistband. He couldn't run and he didn't have to, he just remembered our faces then summoned us down to the principals office. During our lunch period, teachers stood in each corner of the cafeteria, monitoring our activity and to ensure that no one left the cafeteria before the bell rang.

During the end of the lunch period we lined up at the cafeteria door in anticipation of recess. We pushed back-and-forth against the cafeteria doors refusing to obey the demands of the teachers yelling "back away from the doors". One teacher rushed upstairs to the principals office. Within seconds someone yelled 'here come, Mr. Lackey!'. Mr. Lackey, walking as fast as his 350 pound body would allow. Once he got close to the cafeteria doors, he ripped his belt from around His waist, dragging his 60 inch belt on the floor, he yelled out.

"Get back!, Get back!"

Uncontrollably swinging his belt.

"Get back! Get back! Get back!".

He yelled, as he charged forward swinging violently at our heads. The young female teachers stood back smiling at Mr. Lackey admiringly as if he had accomplished a great feat. When in reality all he did was bully a bunch of kids.

All the kids fell back in the cafeteria scrambling for their seats. Within seconds Mr. Lackey had total control of the cafeteria. He walked up and down the cafeteria, belt dangling from his hand dragging along the cafeteria floor.

 "Now don't get out of your chairs until I tell you to".

Latching his belt back around his waist, struggling to find the belt loops, he patrolled up and down the middle row of tables with a mean and sinister look on his face. No one dared to move a muscle.

The recess bell rang, but we remain silently in our seats, minutes later we were lined against a wall in an orderly fashion, then escorted to the playground for 30 minutes of outdoor activity. The playground was virtually free of exercise equipment with one basketball rim and all the running space we can tolerate. There were no organized activities or foot races, we ran around loosely on the playground while the more mature boys leaned against the fence posturing, trying to look cool in front of the young girls. I couldn't run too far, jump and play too hard because my shoes were in total disrepair.

My socks hung freely from the bottom of my shoes, the asphalt ripped holes in the toes of my socks. The bottom of my shoes had holes the size of a quarter. If I forgot to line My shoes with cardboard my socks would eventually stick embarrassingly out of the bottom of my shoes.

I thought having tattered clothing was normal, it just meant that little boys were rough, seeing how I can't remember consistently having nice shoes or clothes. I understood my mother was doing the best she could, because though she never had any financial help from my father. She often took us shopping the month before school began. She allowed us to choose our clothes for the school year then place them on layaway.

I was happy for the moment dreaming about the first day of school and being all dressed up in my new clothes. But it never came into fruition. The clothing I selected was substantially reduced to two pairs of pants and two shirts. All the other kids seemed to be dress for success for the first day of school. The smell of new jeans and patent leather shoes was as common on the first day of school as the old black chalkboards and substitute teachers that wouldn't last more then the first part of the year.

School #60 was only a little more than a mile away from my house, but the winter months proved to be challenging. I had to line the sole of my shoes with cardboard to prevent the snow from dampening my socks. I couldn't feel the cold air that chapped my lips or froze my partially exposed toes because I was having too much fun diving in the snow and throwing snowballs. By the time I got to school my clothes were completely saturated. I didn't even noticed the snow that had made its way through the holes on the bottom of my badly worn sneakers that were held together by cardboard to line the inside and tape across the front lips of my shoes. This invention was handed down to me by my older brother Rayford. Like me he had to be creative with shoe and clothes repair. Denton didn't have this problem, my mother made sure he had adequate clothing, and shoes because he lived in the presence of my grandparents.

The winters are unforgiving, and was even colder when we couldn't afford oil for the furnace. The huge three bedroom house was difficult to heat and we often found ourselves huddled in the kitchen in front of the stove, wrapped in blankets trying stay warm. Sooner or later I had to adjourn to my bed where the ice covered the windows, seeping its way inside the window frame rendering a perfectly frosted circle decorating the inside of the window and making a statement," winter has arrived".

The cold pockets of air rushed through the bathroom purposely missing the empty space my brother once occupied. The absence of my brother Rayford left the bedroom even more cold and uncomfortable. Most of the time I was scared half to death, lying in the bed staring at the attic door. I stared at the door so long, psychologically the door knob begin to turn and I would flee downstairs in a rage trying to escape the ghost that traveled to the dark crevices of the unoccupied spaces in our house.

My sisters slept comfortably through the night, because they had one another and they were always at home. My sister Sherry was known to patrol downstairs around the kitchen and living room, ensuring the doors were locked before settling down for the night. She was considered an unofficial security guard and a second mother to all of us. She had a guitar she didn't play, and a bicycle she seldom rode. She was a collector of things, kind of a young hoarder but her intentions was to reap the benefits overtime by keeping her possessions in perfect condition and allowing them to age into antiques. The idea of possessing an antique guitar went out the window as quick as the thought came into her head.

One day Sherry and Rayford were having an argument over a bet that Rayford couldn't drink an entire bottle of hot sauce. Rayford drank the entire bottle of hot sauce, but had a violent reaction afterwards. He ran through the house drinking bucket after bucket of water. The water couldn't come out of the tap fast enough, his mouth was on fire. Sherry laughed so hard tears ran down her face.

Rayford followed behind her wanting Sherry to pay him for the bet. She laughed and laughed as he followed her up and down the steps trying to requisition his pay. "Stop following me, I'm not paying you anything." She said,The more she laughed he became very agitated. Rayford without thinking shoved her towards the steps. She tumbled a few feet, and before he could react, she grabbed her guitar and bashed him over there with it, then fled up the stairs. Rayford struggled and staggered around the living room trying to free yourself from the guitar strings. Sherry locked herself in the bedroom and didn't come out until late in the evening. Rayford eventually calmed down and disappeared onto the streets from which he came.

Spring was always a pleasant time of the year, fresh grass birthing in the front yard, while the final signs of winter flushed their ways down the sewers. Christmas was over and all the holiday sweets were gone. My sweet tooth was in high gear and my pockets were beginning to feel the effects of juvenile poverty. My entrepreneur spirit shifted into high gear. I began to think of ways I could earn money by cutting grass or picking up trash in people's yards. I didn't own a lawn mower so that idea was short-lived, it was just another obstacle in front of me and the candy store.

$\mathcal{J}$ohn

While waiting for another idea to pop into my head I sat down on the green plush grass of one of the big houses, five minutes into my thinking, the sun was suddenly eclipsed by a large shallow blocking the sun rays and interrupting my casual tanning session. I tilted my head backward and elevated my eyes in the direction of the human eclipse. There he was, a six-foot tall graying white man with a kind face and a gentle voice.

He said, "Where do you lived?"

I replied. "Across the alley from you".

Then I asked.

"Would you like your grass cut?" In a high tone overly anxious voice.

(John) "Do you have a lawn mower"?

(Mikey) "No",

(John) "How will you cut my grass if you don't have a lawn mower?"

(Mikey) "With your lawn mower"

He then stuck out his over encompassing hand (John) "my name is John".

I shook his hand, his fingers were so large and long, he reminded me of the giant I once saw at the state fair grounds. John's hand smothered my seven-year-old hand as it sunk into his palm.

(Mikey) "my name is Michael but my brothers and sisters call me Mikey".

I followed him to his back yard and was surprised at how well the lawn was maintained. The lawnmower was shoved in a corner of his well organized garage, covered with spider webs and rust invading the wheels and blades.

I was confused at how he could possibly maintain his yard so well with a dilapidated, antiquated lawn mower with a single big rusted blade in the middle, flanked by one tire on each side. The yard was really big so I charged $3.00 to cut the front and two dollars to cut the back. I began my auspicious chore cutting the grass at 10: am, and I finished cutting the grass by 2pm that afternoon. I was totally exhausted, my shirt was cover with sweat and the palms of my hands were painfully red. As I slumped to the ground I realized that the lawn mower was older than it appeared, the blade was dull and duck tape was holding the handles together.

John came back outside; his face was red from laughing as if he had been watching the Red Skeleton show. Instead, he had watched me painfully cutting the grass the whole time. He invited me into his house to celebrate the completion of my first job. As I entered his house I was amazed at the volume of books that lined his book shelf and how clean and unlived in his house looked.

I cruised from one room to another amazed at how perfectly the boarders of the walls were trimmed with dark thick wood matching the wooden floors and bookshelves. The walls were spotless and the furniture untouched as though no child had ever occupied the space. Hundreds of books sat undisturbed and perfectly placed in volume order on the book shelfs.

I was only a child but I could see that these were law books. I was just in eyeshot of John, staring as he opened a wood grain cigar box. I stood quietly behind him as he took out a stack of one dollar bills. My eyes bulged as I thought to myself, "That must be $20 in cash, he must be rich". John paid me four dollars and some orange slices from his candy dish.   I took my new found wealth home and sat admiringly in front my four sisters and counted my earnings, 10 times, in 10 different ways. My siblings were surely jealous of my new wealth.   I didn't know allot about money, all I knew was that Now & Laters cost five cents a pack and I could get 20 packs for one dollar, nothing else mattered. After counting my four dollars over and over I ran one block to the penny store ready to turn my pot of gold into a pot of candy.

A man that has a 1000 friends has not one friend to spare, a man that has one enemy will meet him everywhere.

 As I turned the corner a boy leaped from behind the bushes, and grabbed me by my shirt, with his fist raised high in the air.

(Bully) "give me all your money".

 I was nervous, and he could see the fear in my eyes. Up to this point in my life my brother Denton was the only one to make me willfully submit to him, but I knew that my brother would not cause me any harm and if he did I could call out to mother for help. This kid was twice my size and had a mean look in his eyes.

(Mikey) "This money belongs to my mother, I was sent to the store to get some milk".

Another boy approached as the bully clenched my shirt, he couldn't have been more than six years old.

(Enron) "leave him alone stinky man, let him go" The boy let me pass.

(Bully) " There is a toll charge for crossing this side of the street".

I was distraught even though that wasn't my first time facing bullies, but I always had the backing of friends or my brothers. Unfortunately this time my support system had collapsed. Rayford was always chasing girls and Denton lived with my grandparents on the West side of town. The corner of 30th and Delaware and cutting between houses was the shortest route to the store and there was no way of avoiding running into my would be assailant again.

I was forced to use an alternate route, walking between houses then dashing down the alley to the store, little difference did that make, the bully hung around the corner at his cousins house directly across the street from the store. If I was to have any peace I knew I would have to fight this guy.   As my luck would have it my mother unknowingly demanded increasingly that I go to the store and buy butter and evaporated milk, that she forgot to get it at the grocery store the day before. I ran to the corner of 30th and Delaware St, peaked around the corner, to my amazement there was no bully.

I successfully ran these black ops three times before the bully got a glimpse of me. As I scurried across the alley and got partially over the fence, an annoying yell came out of nowhere.

(Bully) "You owe me a day's toll punk, I'm going to get you next time".

While scrambling over the fence my pants leg got caught on the fence, I struggled and pulled as the bully ran closer. I took a deep breath and pulled one final time ripping a hole in the knee of my pants. I was free! I ran so fast, being so excited, I was running free of motion, swinging my arms back-and-forth not even noticing the small paper bag began ripping in shreds. The butter and milk flung in the air landing in the puddles of rainwater on street.

The bully ran to the fence, kicking the fence and screaming.

" That's the last time you're going to get away from me, next time you're going to pay double."

I stayed inside the house for the next three days rehearsing fighting scenes after watching the Green hornet. I practiced day in and day out in my bedroom, training myself for the day I was to face the bully again. My cash flow of $4-$5 every two weeks had come to a sudden halt. I had been without candy for four days now and I was beginning to have withdrawals. Visions of grape, watermelon, banana, lemon and chocolate Now & Laters were dancing in my head.

So I ventured backed out in the world of entrepreneurial ship. My first stop was at a huge home that had slave quarters in the back of the home and an oversized yard. The house sat one house from the top of the hill of 31st and Pennsylvania Street. The yard was so big I thought for sure I was on a plantation. The grass was so green and rich and beautiful, I was going blind from seeing and smelling what I thought were acres of grass. I was like a deer caught in the headlights, total burnout was set in place. The thought of cutting this grass made me sick to my stomach. But my desire for candy was even greater than my desire not to cut the yard. Up-and-down back-and-forth across the yard. The grass was so rich my white sneakers had turned green in color. The lawn mower choked every few feet from the thick richness of the lawn.

After a long day of cutting the over-sized yard, I sat on the curve drinking from the water hose that stretched from the mansion down to the sidewalk. It was the best tasting water I had ever tasted at that moment, but something was still amiss. I needed my sugar fix. I had to have my Now & Laters, and for celebratory purposes I was going to buy hostess cupcakes with white filling in the middle. The last thing on my list of cavity makers was a pack of chocolate Now & Later's.

The word on the street was that there were no chocolate Now & Laters on the market anymore. I had to have them. By 1 o'clock I journeyed down the street to the store, I was too tired to take shortcuts, or to allow anything to diverge me from the thoughts of chocolate Now & Laters that swirled around my head like marbles in the ping-pong machine. I knew I wouldn't have a clear thought in my head until I could taste the soothing chocolate flavored of Now & Laters flowing freely throughout my mouth.

I walked in the variety store, slapped one dollar bill on the counter and demanded 20 packs of chocolate Now & Laters. I didn't even allow the cashier to bags the Now & Laters, I shoved nineteen packs in my pocket, dismantling one pack and shoving all eight pieces in my mouth at the same time. The juices flowed freely as I walked out of the store in candy heaven, but as fate would have it, the bully showed up, fist in air.

(Bully) "where's my toll Punk!".

He ran across the street stopping me in my tracks, but I was too tired to listen to his hyperbole and wasn't about to surrender my earnings. So I jumped into my boxing pose, energized by the chocolate sugar juices. I wasn't willing to share or surrender, not one Now & Later.

I was in Now & Later heaven. For a brief second I lost myself and yelled.

"I ain't giving you nothing!"

The bully ran back to the other side of the street.

(Bully) " I will fix you!".

I never had another problem from him and didn't see him again for two years. I went on that year making friends with one other kid that live two houses down from my home. He was much younger than I, at least three years younger, but I found him to be very nice and pleasant to be around. We ran and frolicked around as kids do, diving in the grass and running through the rain bare footed. As fate would have it my usual luck would show it's ugly face.

*A*n apple a day won't keep the doctors away

The torrential rains came to a sudden halt leaving puddles and puddles of water flooding in the streets, nearly creeping its way to my front door. Being Mikey, I couldn't help but roll my jeans up and jump into the ankle high water. My sisters stood on the porch watching as I ran up and down the street like Salmon swimming upstream. Suddenly there was a pricking sensation on the bottom of my foot. I noticed a trail of blood stretching at least a half block behind me.

I drag my foot slowly through the water, limping my way home. With every step I was in agonizing pain. A half broken pop bottle had lodged deep into the center of my foot. Maybe it was a sign from God I thought. The half broken pop bottle happened to have held my favorite drink on the planet. It was a grape Nehi-high soda. I squeeze my foot trying to stop the bleeding and within seconds the palms of my hands were filled with blood. Tiana's undiagnosed hypersensitivity what's activated by her trigger for chaos. She began screaming bloody hell, causing everyone else in the house to panic, propelling Sherry to my rescue.

Sherry laid me on the couch and wrapped a towel around my foot, but this time before she could call an ambulance my mother walked through the door.

(Mother) "What the hell did you do now Boy"? "Dammit he needs stitches!" she said.

And within an hour I was lying on the backseat of my auntie's Buick slowly dehydrating from her plastic seat covers. Quickly I was snatched from the car and placed on a gurney. I stared at the ceilings and the white hospital walls as I was shoved into an operating room. This time the room had big silver blinding lights staring me in the face.

A young white man came into the room and begin pressing hard on the bottom of my foot." Lie still" he said, I have to palpate to see if there's more glass. Every time he touched my foot I screamed and kicked bloody hell.

"It's just a cotton ball" he said, rubbing it on the bottom of my foot.

The alcohol burned and stung like a pack of bumblebees. He raised a needle in the air, fluid dripping from its tip, I jumped off the bed and hobble down the hallway on one foot, and suddenly I was picked up by a large black man resembling the character on the spic and span bottle named Mr. clean. He aggressively pinned me to the bed. I was frozen like a popsicle, too afraid to move. I could barely breathe with his 250 pound body lying across my small, 50 pound frame.

The doctor shoved the long needle in the bottom of my foot three times before grabbing a hook and threading it with 3-0 silk to sew the gashing whole on my foot. I spent the next two weeks getting piggy back rides from my sister Marica. Before I could return to school my mother decided she needed to remove the stitches from my foot. I never saw the bottom my foot and didn't know there were so many stitches to be removed. I thought if she waited long enough the stitches would fall out by themselves. There I was once again screaming and kicking bloody hell. Removing the stitches didn't really hurt, I just associated the metal tweezers with the 6 inch needle at the bottom of my foot. The following Monday I was back in school and in full swing of my mischievous behavior. Once again our lunch program had changed and we were required to pay for lunch, this time rather than bring our lunch to school. We couldn't afford to purchase our lunch or bring lunch, so the principal gave us permission to walk home for lunch. It took about 15 minutes to walk home and 15 minutes back to the school. Lunch was only an hour including recess time. By the time we made it back to school, recess had ended and we were forced to go directly to class. We made it home just in time to remove the potatoes from the refrigerator and allow them to cook for 10 minutes before heading back to school. The potatoes were still raw and I often went back to school as hungry as when I left.

I couldn't take it anymore! After two months of eating raw potatoes I was starving to death. I was only 50 pounds soaking wet and couldn't afford to lose anymore weight. I was bound to come up with a plan. So I ran ahead of my sisters Tiana and Marica, I thought if I could begin the cooking process the potatoes wouldn't be raw and I wouldn't go back to school hungry. So I busted through the front door locking it behind me with the purpose of slowing my sisters down. I filled the pan up to the rim with cooking oil and turned the fire up as high as I could get it. The grease was boiling in no time, smoke billowing from the pan. That was my cue, I grabbed the potatoes soaking water from the refrigerator and threw a stack of potatoes into the grease. The fire shot out of the pan in a roaring blaze scorching the ceiling. I knew this was a bad idea, so I quickly turned the fire off and put a top over the skillet to douse the fire.

The skillet handle was red hot, I was a quick thinker so I opened the back door, grabbed the skillet with a towel and tossed the entire pan, grease, french fries and all into the backyard. As my luck would have it, the first one through the door was Tianna,

" Oh, I'm going to tell mom on you, you tried to burn the house down".

(Marica) "Boy what are you trying to do, now we don't have lunch."

I hunched my shoulders, thinking to myself,

"It wasn't a total lost" because we never got to eat anyway.

Once we arrived back at school my class was loaded onto a buss for a short field trip to the Children's Museum. I sat quietly on the buss thinking about my punishment I had to face after school. I could feel the force of someone staring at the from the back row of the buss. Her eyes were burning a hole in the back of my head. I turned to look in her direction and her pop bottle glasses threw me into to a frantic. For a minute I thought I was reliving the Stella Glass episode, but it was only May, a girl with a profound crush on me. Her clothes were tether like that of a foster child. Her red coat was worn beyond repair and her hair was matted to her head with two braids that stuck out of the side of her head like devil horns. She followed me around the museum the entire day, not being more than two feet from me at any given time. When I turned to look at a display, their she stood within kissing distance. She breath down my neck like a fire breathing dragon with her lips coming dangerously close to kissing me. I was put off by her stocking ability and her denial of personal space. But as distasteful and annoying as her presences was it couldn't distract me from thoughts of being beaten with a razor strap.

I spent the next four hours of my day anticipating the whipping I knew I had coming. I sat in class staring at the clock, my teacher pontificated nonstop, but I couldn't hear a word she said. All I could think about was the leather razor strap ripping through my skin, leaving marks across my back with every swing.

Finally the bell rung, I was the last one to get my coat from the cloak hall and the last one to form a line along the staircase waiting for the school doors to open. All the kids ran out to freedom. I wasn't running or jumping because I knew I would be running into a beating. My sisters ran home ahead of me, I stayed back and watched them play as I slipped down to the alley of forbidden territory were the bully lived.

I was no longer in fear of his presence, I was only in fear of what I knew was about to happen so I walked the long way home, circling the block where I lived, going up and down the alley and into the apartment where Peanuts live. Eventually I walked down the alley towards my house. From a distance I could see Bryce's white convertible Buick coupe in the driveway where a garage once stood. I stopped by the first tree that I saw and broke a long switch from one of its branches, then stripped it of its leaves. I stepped in the door. My eyes bugged out of my head as I peaked around the corner.

He knew I was coming, so he stood there as my eyes looked up and locked onto his unshaved face.

" Get upstairs and take them off!" He said.

I stood in my room butt naked waiting for the beating I knew would come. With every step he made up the staircase my body cringed in fear. I stuck my arm out handing him the switch.

" You won't be needing that" he said.

Folding the belt in half then popping the belt together one time scaring me to death and making me cry before the first lashing. He swung freely, striking me uncontrollably, hitting me in unfamiliar places, putting his 157 pounds behind each blow onto my 50 pound frame. I screamed and yelled bloody hell I thought for sure my mother would have stepped in the room to see what's wrong but she never uttered a word because Bryce was the man of the house and this is the way he disciplined kids. But there was one small problem, I wasn't his kid. In fact they weren't even married.

I never cooked again and we never had to walk home for lunch again. My mother became very creative with her finances and somehow she was able to give each of us .20 cents for lunch, allowing us to eat with the rest of the kids in the cafeteria.

Throughout the school years our lunch programs would change. Sometimes we were required to bring a lunch in brown paper bags and the next year we were required to pay .20 cents for hot and cold lunch served in the cafeteria. In the following year we were required to bring a lunch once again and by this time most kids had a metal lunch box with cartoon characters on the box and a thermos inside for soup or some type of drink. Most of the time my lunch box only contained one sandwich. The other kids in the classroom seemed to have more food than they could eat.

One kid in particular (Eddie) sat next to me in the cafeteria, every chance he got he display his wealth of chips, sandwiches, cookies, fruit, and a soft drink of his choice. His lunchbox was so full it was spilling over with food. He proudly opened it wide for everyone to see. I open my lunch box just wide enough to remove my sandwich, take a bite then slipped my sandwich back into the box. I took a bite every five minutes trying to make my sandwich last throughout the lunch period. Not only did Eddie have an overly adequate amount of food, he always wore new clothes on the first day of school. I did not understand it, how someone could be so privileged while others struggle horribly. I was a good kid, at least I thought so. The only troubles I ever caused were troubles for myself.

I believe that I deserve better, but I knew it wasn't up to me. Being poor was one thing, having other students knowing you're poor was something totally different. A lot of the children at my school could be mean and spiteful. One day I didn't have clean underwear to wear to school, so I went bottomless. Unfortunately for me, one of the kids noticed and told everyone in the class. I was totally embarrassed. Not having clean underwear wasn't my mother's fault. The nocturnal monster appeared just about every morning right before I awoke. I hid my underwear under the mattress trying not to be discovered until Saturday morning during laundry day. My bedwetting went mostly undetected because Denton lived across town with my grandparents.

Bryce was tired after driving his truck all day and never came into my bedroom unless it was brought to his attention by Denton. For some reason my brother didn't like me. I don't know if it was because I was an annoying little brother or because he was forced to live with my grandparents and felt that my mother gave him up rather than giving me up. For whatever reason he continuously tried to get me hurt.

One day he was playing football with his friends. I sat on a telephone pole on the sidelines cheering them on as they played the game of football.

" Can I play?" I said." No, you're too little".

His friend Bruce replied. I sat there momentarily depressed and feeling rejected until an older gentleman interrupted their game.

" This little boy and I will take on both teams". The man said.

"We get to run the ball first," he said, handing me the ball.

" Get behind me and hold onto my belt".

He took off running shoving my brother and his friends to the ground, I laughed hysterically as I ran across the goal line smiling from ear to ear.

He said. "come on we're going to go again".

I grabbed onto the back of his belt, and off we went from one end of the field to the other, scoring touchdown after touchdown. I laughed heartily as my brother and his friends lay on the ground defeated. The man tossed them the football, then waved goodbye. Before I could return to set on the telephone pole, Denton and Bruce simultaneously

Said," come on you can play".

They immediately handed me the ball to run, and for some strange reason I got around all of them and scored a touchdown. It was beautiful! Bruce became enraged.

" That was just luck, do it again, I dare you to run it again".

I was having too much fun, smiling from ear to ear. Denton and Bruce walked to the edge of the field, having a secret conversation. I was handed the ball and off I went, blockers in front of me, then all of a sudden my blockers disappeared. Bruce came charging full steam ahead, he hit me so hard, I tumbled in the air three times before landing on a phone pole. Their I lay lifelessly on my back with my neck bent over the phone pole and my arms sprawled out on each side away of my body. He thought for sure he killed me." Mikey, Mikey" he said, in a panicking state.

He even cried a little, thinking he killed me. When I regained consciousness, Denton said.

"He'll be okay, stand up Mikey, and run the ball again.

I did as instructed and they freely let me make touchdown after touchdown, cheering me alone the away, temporarily rebuilding my confidence. I was an internally tough kid, nothing could stop me from having fun or being mischievous, not even being knocked unconscious. It began to rain and everyone grew tired of playing football, I was still re-covering from my state of unconsciousness and wasn't up to running another football; therefore I decided to immediately ran home. Along the way I ran into Sherry standing in the alley holding her bicycle, known as a bus. The bicycle had two huge rubber tires and a thick heavy frame. The bike was called a bus because the tires were so thick they made noise as they turned. Sherry parked the bike by the back steps then ventured into the house.

I quickly jumped on the bike and down the alley I raced off. Sherry chased me around the parking lot of the flower shop, screaming,

"Bring back my bike!"

I laughed as I rode around the parking lot in circles, laughing harder as Sherry tried to grab the back of the seat. Each time she got close, I would speed up throwing rain wa-ter on her from the oversize tires on the bike. I ride a few feet before slamming on the brakes causing the tire to slide sideways. Sherry became enraged.

" Bring back my bike, you black punk" she said.

I continued to make her chase me. One thing I didn't realize about her bike, it was a kickback, meaning, if you didn't apply the break at the right time, the petal would kick back forward.

I stood up on the bike to increase my speed so I could slide once I slammed on the brakes. I had just reached optimal speed as I stood up I slammed on the brakes. The brake pedal kicked forward and hurled me over the handlebars into the air. Once again I was flipping in circles in mid air. I splashed down in a puddle of rain water, saturating me from head to toe.

" That's what you get" Sherry said.

She picked her bike up, grinning, laughing and snorting her way back home.

I limped my way back home and lay quietly on the couch trying to catch the breath that was just knocked out of me.

Tiana said." Mama and Bryce left a bottle of Kool-Aid on the table, there is some left over, you can have it".

She walked over to the table and poured me a tall glass of grape drink from the bottle sitting in the center of the table.

"This is an odd looking kool-Aid container" I said to myself.

Tiana was my buddy and if I couldn't trust her who can I trust, but she wouldn't explain what the label name meant, (Wild Irish Rose) I decide to drink it anyway.

"Drink it all" Tiana said. "Don't waste it drink the entire glass".

The glass was just about toppling over with Wild Irish Rose running down the side. I had no problem drinking Kool-Aid, no matter how full the glass was so, I choked it down with one swift swallow.

By the time I got to the bottom of the glass I was just about crawling up the steps. The world was spinning out of control, and my eyes rolled freely in my head like a bag of ten cent marbles. Tiana grabbed the empty bottle as she ran past me up the stairs with bottle in hand to present the empty bottle to my mother." I'm going to have Bryce beat your ass" my mother said.

For some reason I wasn't scared of the empty threat. I crawled into my bed and passed out for the night. Bryce came to the door, belt in hand. His small frame filled the entry to the doorway and for the first time I wasn't intimidated by him, he stood there calling out my name.

" Mikey, Mikey, you hear me boy."

I turn my head toward him barely able to open my eyes. Then I passed out. For the first time we had a connection, he understood me just for that brief moment in time. He knew what it was like to be stone cold drunk on your face. So he walked away and never spoke of it again. Within a week Bryce was leaving for mechanics school. He would be gone approximately two weeks to a month for training. Miraculously once Bryce left my biological father appear. Although he hadn't been in my life for years I found it refreshing to have him in the house again.

Within two weeks time, my biological father departed and Bryce returned from his mechanics training. I didn't understand relationships and although my mother told me not to talk about my father in front of Bryce I thought it would be nice to share the fact my father stayed with us while he was away at Mechanics School. Within 10 minutes my mother and Bryce was in a full toe to toe fight. Bryce was very fortunate my mother didn't have a gun or he would've become just another victim of self defense by anger.

I could hear furniture moving and being thrown around the bedroom, they were having a 'donnybrook' (A free for all, knock-down drag out fight). My mother ran downstairs and Bryce came down hurling behind her raving mad. The fight continued into the front room escalating at a fever pitch. Bryce pick my mother up and body slammed her onto the floor. I ran into the kitchen and grabbed a fork. My mother sat lifelessly on the floor trying to recover from the body slam. Bryce reached down and grabbed her by the face then punched her in the eye with his fist. Sherry went hysterically frantic while dialing 911. I stood there tightly clinging onto a fork, tears streaming down my face, feeling defenseless. Bryce stood towering over my mother yelling and screaming.

 I was so traumatized I temporarily went death, then the police rushed in and wrestled Bryce to the ground. Within the short seven year span of my life, the police intervene twice, busting in my house and arresting someone I knew. This time I didn't care if I would ever see Bryce again. Later that evening, an hour after the episode had ended, my grandfather came over to our house. Barely able to walk, he had three Butcher knives wrapped in newspaper." Where is he?" he said, as my grandmother ushered him to the nearest chair. Somehow I felt a little reassured even though my grandfather was too old to fight a young 30 year old man.

My grandmother knew we didn't have food to eat and had the wisdom to bring us a bag of potatoes and stick of butter to assuage my mother's grief. The assuage lasted about as long as it took my grandparents to get back into their car. My grandparents were poor financially but rich in spirit. They couldn't afford to help out much but the small amount of food they gave us left us better off then we were before they arrived.

 Holding the bag of raw potatoes in one hand she waved good bye just before preparing dinner. She stood behind the stove peeling and frying potatoes, silently crying to herself. I stood squeamishly quiet in the corner of the living room and watched her cry as she cooked what would be our dinner. In a flash she made her way upstairs jumping in the tub to begin the ablution process. The sound of the bath water seemed to splash around for an hour. I guess it provided her anodyne in her time of need.

 I know she was lost in thought, hurt and embarrassed all rolled into one. I couldn't help but feel sorry for her, and I vowed to destroy my step father if he ever hurt her again. Within a weeks time Bryce was back in the house, every time I looked at him I want to stick a fork straight in his back, but I knew he was too strong and would just disarm me. So I stayed as far away from him as I could get. The end of another school year was approaching fast. Denton returned home for the summer, and I knew he couldn't wait to tell Bryce when the nocturnal monster appeared thrusting me back into a life of torment.

Denton took pleasure in monitoring my every move. Every morning as I awoke, Denton stood by the bed waiting for me to get up. Sometimes I could turn the mattress over in the twilight hours of the morning. After two or three times of safely getting away with wetting the bed, he knew it was too good to be true, so he caught on to what I was doing. He jumped out of the bed first thing in the morning, pushed me out of the way and flipped the mattress over displaying the huge spot left by the nocturnal monster. He ran down the hall to my mothers room and summoned Bryce.

" Now you're going to get it" he said, laughing to himself.

I could hear the popping of the razor strap as Bryce's bare feet slapped against the naked wooden floors.

" Take them off". He said.

 Bryce stared at me as though he was trying to intimidate me. I didn't bat an eye while stripping from head to toe. Denton ran downstairs snickering and laughing to himself as though this was his greatest achievement. Bryce grabbed me by the arm once again. The swings of the belt were a little more uncontrollable and violent. The whipping lasted a little longer but I didn't move a muscle our flex a bit.

Crazy like a Fox

It wasn't long before a new family moved on the block, and occupied the large four bed-room house next to the apartment complex. I was surprised at how big the family was. There were so many kids, that the mother put a chain around the refrigerator and se-cure it with a heavy duty pad lock.

In a weeks time I became friends with three of the younger children all near my age. Ja-son was the oldest of the three that I hung around with. His younger brother Meyers went everywhere Jason went kind of like my brother and I but Jason welcome Meyers presence. His sister Anita was just as crazy as Jason and Meyer. They played games far more dangerous than I would ever consider. They climbed to the top of the attic and jumped off the roof using umbrellas as parachutes.

I climbed up to the attic, and looked out the window, I got so dizzy I fell back inside on the floor. I didn't participate in their parachute jumps but I spent many hours playing with them in their backyard. They enjoyed my company so much they invited me to go to the laundromat with them at 8 o'clock the next morning. Trash bags after trash bag, after trash bag were loaded into the back of their dilapidated station wagon. The hinges on the door let out a loud irritating squeak. Once the door slammed closed, particles of rust fell in my lap. I quickly became disenchanted with the idea of helping to wash all those clothes. So I declined the offer to go to laundromat.

Jason's mother made me a special offer, she promised me ice cream if I would go to the laundromat with them.

"How delightful" I thought.

I quickly ran home and begged my mother for the chance to do a good deed by going to the laundromat and helping someone. She didn't even bat an eye, she waved her hand bye and off I went five blocks in a 20-year-old station wagon loaded down with 10 hefty bags of laundry. The laundromat was jam packed with people. I saw no foreseeable future in ever getting a washer. Every family seemed as though they had several times the laundry we had, as if they were washing for an entire army not a family. We had to wait at least an hour before we got one washer. So the conquest for a washer was on. Each of us took a corner of the laundromat, once a washer became available we flag their mother down and she would come running with a garbage bag of clothes.

Three hours into the trip I began to get bored and complacent. I was ready to go home, even if I had to walk. I stared at the five bags of unwashed laundry, opening and closing my eyes wishing they were washed and put away. I knew I would be in for a long night. Anita and Meyer tried to keep me occupied playing freeze tag in front of the laundromat, running up and down the street.

Every time I passed the laundromat window, I saw five or six washers and dryers operating at the same time, and there were still three bags of unwashed laundry staring back at me through the window. I couldn't believe it, it was approaching 6 o'clock in the evening and they were just beginning to dry the last five bags of clothes. Finally 8 o'clock arrive. We all gladly piled in the car heading home, but first we made a pit stop to pick up some ice cream.

"Oh yes'"

 I thought, smiling from ear to ear, with visions of large bowls of ice cream dancing in my head.

Their mother got out of the car bristly walked into the store returning with a small bag, small enough to fit in the palm of a small child's hand. I thought to myself.

" This can't be ice cream, ice cream comes in large cartons or large plastic tubs. She must have the ice cream in the refrigerator at home".

We arrived at the house and quickly unloaded the car in anticipation of a large bowl of ice cream. Jason's mother placed a paper bag on the table then pulled out a small quart of ice cream. She took a knife and cut small slits of ice cream and delicately placed each piece on a paper towel. My jaw hit the floor, I didn't want to show disappointment on my face but I just couldn't hide it.

"What the hell is this, before Abraham Lincoln shit, I thought to myself".

I was at that damn laundromat for 12 hours and this is all I got. I Grabbed my ice cream and made my way back down the dimly lit street. I was only three houses away and within two bites the ice cream was gone before my foot hit the first step to our house. I had never been so disappointed in my life, I would never fall for such a con again. Just like my mother they were preparing their household for Thanksgiving. This was the first time my family would all sit at the same dinner table, including Denton and Rayford. I couldn't believe it. I smiled the entire time, and they both spent the night. I slept well that night and I didn't even wet the bed next morning.

In the month of December 1968 Christmas had arrived, the most joyous time of year, but the atmosphere was filled with vexation. Martin Luther King was assassinated, tension in this city was at an all-time high. People ran up and down the street, screaming and yelling. My mother told us not to go outside but I snuck out the basement door anyway just to get a peek. People were running and screaming up-and-down 30th St. The glass door to the variety store was kicked completely out. I stared at the Now & Later's behind the untouched glass case. The Now & Laters seemed to call to me.

"Mikey, Mikey, don't you want to pick just one pack?."

Before I could answer the thought in my head the store owner showed up. His head neatly wrapped with a scarf protecting his hair style known as a process.

"Get away from my damn store". He yelled.

As he slipped and slid on the glass, flashlight and gun in hand, making his way to the back of store. I ran back down the block and threw my basement door before my mother could detect I was gone. I saw someone standing in the corner of my basement.

He was a tall black man much bigger than Bryce in height and stature. I ran upstairs to alert my mother. She quickly grabbed a butcher knife. Making our way to the top of the stairs, she flipped on the light switch.

"What are you doing down here?" she asked while the police sirens blasted up and down the block.

" Is that for you?" she asked.

Shaking his head yes.

(Mother) "I'm going to give you three minutes to get out of here, and when I come back downstairs you better be gone or I'm going to call the police and let them know you're in my basement".

The man agreed and my mother went back upstairs locking the basement door behind her. I stood in the kitchen and listened for him to leave. I guess she thought it was his imbroglio not hers. My mother made her way back down to check the basement and lock the basement door that leads to the outside. I never told her it was my fault the door was unlocked or the small fact that I ran a block and a half away to watch the riot unfold around the corner from my home.

1968 was so crazy, I scarcely recall any of the gifts I received other than a set of Rocking Socking Robots. It was the year my grandfather walked into the veterans Hospital with walking pneumonia and never walked out. Later that month he passed away. I had just turned eight years old on December 4, the day before my grandmother's birthday. It was cold and the ice covered every open crevice on the street. It was my first time seeing my entire family micro and macro in one place. It was a joyous time but a sad occasion for me to see my family.

I didn't understand the sadness that filtered throughout the room. I sat in the fourth row watching my grandfather looking placid in his nondescript casket, wearing a freshly pressed blue suit. Sounds of lachrymose sadness echoed throughout the mortuary. I stared it all the faces of my family members, my cousins, aunties and uncles, brothers and sisters. It was unbelievable, we were all in one place for the first time. We stayed for two hours then back home we went to prepare for school the next day. I was scared half to death once again.

I was all alone in a big creepy empty room. I was now trapped by the vision of my grandfather lying peacefully in his casket. I scarcely remembered the belt whipping in the unfinished statement about swiping icing from the cake. I wasn't fortunate enough to spend quality time with my grandfather, instead he was born to soon and I too late to form any type of rapport. I scarcely knew of his existence and the fact that he volunteered to watch us while my mother was in the hospital spawning my sister into the New World. But I couldn't get the image of him lying in his casket out of my head.

I lay in bed that night wide awoke listening to the settling of the house and the ice cold air scratching vigorously with its invisible icy claws at the slowly rotting wooden frame temporarily stabilizing the window. Slowly I dozed off, three hours later I was awakened by the forces of nature. For the first time my body summoned me to get up and go to the bathroom. I wiped my eyes trying to refocus my vision readjusting to the light. Standing in front of the toilet I felt re-assured the nocturnal monster wouldn't have a chance to re-turn this night.

As I started to urinate slow footsteps began coming up stairs. I stopped urinating mid stream, jumped in the bed and buried myself deep beneath my covers. The sound of foot steps stopped, a window closed then down the hallway of the steps went. I thought for sure it was spectral visit by my grandfather walking up the stairs securing the house. The image of him lying in his casket and the sound of footsteps threw me into an over-whelming panic. I shook violently beneath my blanket.

I was too scared to even peak from beneath the covers, so, I lay there until I dozed off and was awaken by the nocturnal monster early the next morning. Bryce walked into the room, looked at my urine fill mattress.

(Bryce) "Boy you need to get your lazy butt up and go to the bathroom" he said.

Then off he went at four in the morning to work. Bryce had one good quality, he was a functioning alcoholic. No matter how much he drank the night before he was able to get up the next morning at 4 AM and go to work. Other than that I thought he was pretty useless.

He never spoke when he walked into the house. He didn't care whether I got hurt or went to the hospital, he barely helped pay any bills and he was no type of role model for me or my brothers. He lived his life the way he wanted too, which was to hang out on Indiana Avenue, 12 hours a day drinking with friends after work. I didn't understand why it took my mother so long to become aware of and grow weary of his behavior. He was in it for himself and no one else.

He pushed his head of the household boundaries to the limit. Reclining back in his leather recliner, on Sundays he watched war movies all day long. I sat next to his recliner waiting for him to fall asleep so I could have a chance to watch the wizard of oz that came on once a year the same time every year. As soon as I turned the channel he would awaken and say turn it back. He wasn't even watching the TV but he felt compelled to honor the veterans who served our country, but he didn't have the courage to honorably complete his tour in the military.

I sat behind him with my back pressed against the wall for another 30 minutes until he decided to reside upstairs. I hurry to flip through the four channels including UHF. And their she was making her way to the land of OZ. Life went on like this for the next month and as you would know it another baby was born, January 1969, my sister Rhianna. She would be the last of the family to be born to this clan, bring our enclave to a total of eight. Another mouth stretching my mothers limited dollars a little farther than they were financially able to go.

$\mathcal{P}$ark Avenue

It was 1969 and we were on the move again, unfortunately this time our house was located right in the heart and soul of the ghetto, (30th and Park Avenue). Once again Sam rented us one of his prized rental properties, a big gray double that provided more space than a young mischievous boy in his preteen years could fathom. The street was very long as though it was two blocks made into one. I wasted no time running up the steps and sorted my way through all the bedrooms. My mother stopped me mid stride and said,

" This back bedroom is yours and your brothers."

I stared at her as though I was a deer caught in headlights.

"Not again, why is it that we always get the bedroom facing the alley".

I was thoroughly discussed, I would've loved to have had the bedroom facing the street, so that I could yell at everyone that pass by or stare out the window at the neighbors sitting on their front porch.

Once again we were fortunate to have our school #76 located four short blocks from our house. The scenic route provided plenty of distractions for a young boy on his way to school, such as Frogs Record Shop, and variety stores that sold my favorite penny candy. We drove the store clerk crazy. It took us 10 minutes to spend .25 cents . Three pieces of candy for one penny.

"Give me two of them, and two of them and three of those and five of them," I said.

By the time I was done naming off all the candy I wanted, my small 6 inch tall bag was spilling over with candy. I quickly doubled back home jamming the overflow of candy underneath my mattress.

Here I stood in a 2800 square-foot home. I was shoved to the back of the house, where I was sure to manifest nightmares while I lay in the bed staring at the closet door. The door cracked open to the attic, displaying its endless flight of stairs that stretched into the abysmal darkness of an on unoccupied and Un-interrupted space. I had no desire to venture up those stairs, there was little comfort when my brother Rayford walked into the room and gladly ran up the steps into the attic and turned on the light displaying the empty room. He pulled me up the steps by my hand.

Rayford said, "See there's nothing here and there's nothing to be afraid of".

I didn't care I snatched my hand away from him and ran down the steps. I knew when the hours of midnight came Rayford would not be home and I would be left to fend for myself in the night and in the morning as the nocturnal monster displayed its ugly head, soaking my bed. Bryce's leather belt would once again strike a devastating blow to my young self-confidence and self-esteem. I was shy and had little friend making capably. I set quietly on the back steps watching the squirrels and the birds play in the backyard looking as though I didn't have a friend in the world.

Rayford noticed I was sitting in the backyard, so he began grabbing bottles and cans. Stacking them on a concrete block in front of the trash can, he called me over and show me how to use the cans and bottles for target practice. Before long, two other boys joined in the rock throwing. Then Rayford quietly walked away as we introduced our-selves and became friends. We were having so much fun the day passed quickly then the universal rule signaled us it was time to go in the house.

The streetlights began to flicker as though they want to come on, that meant we had to go inside the house. I'd be grudgingly walked in the house and to my surprise there Denton stood with his bags in his hands. He was home for the summer and I was glad to see him because that meant I didn't have to spend lonely nights in that huge dark empty grey bedroom all by myself, "So I thought". I was so thrilled that Denton was home I grabbed his bags and carried them upstairs and placed his bags on his bed. I sat curiously by his side as I watched him unpack item by item and place them neatly on the closet shelf.

R espect, crying not an option

This must've been the slowest form of entertainment in the world, my eyelids became heavy as I slid back onto the bed. I was awakened by two kicks to my foot. As I focused my eyes, Denton was pointing at the attic door. I rolled over to my right and there was my favorite knit hat lying at the top of the attic staircase. That hat was my security blanket. I can give you one guess as to how it got there.

I stared at Denton and he looked at me hunching his shoulders and said.

"If you want your hat back, there it is, go get it."

I didn't hesitate for a second, I sprang to my feet and shot up the upstairs like a bullet train riding airlessly on rails, before I knew it the door slammed shut behind me the lock spinning in its chamber, locking me in the dark abyss of the attic.

I screamed bloody hell, kicked and beat on the door. I could hear my mother yelling as she ran down the hallway.

"Let that boy out of the attic!".

She snatched the door open and slapped Denton upside the head. I set idol on the bed trying not to laugh. Denton smirked at me and said.

"I'm going to get you back, punk ".

I was hardly worried, but he got his revenge the next morning, the nocturnal monster showed its ugly face. I had awakened to an ugly and wet situation. Denton stood towering over me smiling as though he had won the lottery.

I knew I was in trouble, Denton ran downstairs like a dog at the racetrack giving Bryce the full run down on my bed wedding activities.

Bryce, "Where's my beltinnate? He yelled, " That damn boy is too lazy to get his ass out of the bed and go to the bathroom".

I knew I wasn't going to convince him that I was a deep sleeper and didn't know I had wet the bed. I woke up and it was there. This was all too confusing, instead of trying to develop me into a successful Business savvy young man he invested his time trying to beat me to a submissive state, something that will never happen because I was born with an internal strength and a resiliency that wouldn't allow me to succumb to psychological or physiological pressure. This innate ability would serve me well later in life.

At that moment I decided I wasn't going to give him the pleasure of seeing me cry or squirm from the flash cutting strikes of his belt. Bryce walked into the room he didn't break stride as he grabbed my arm and violently began swing his belt, once he realized I still had my pants on he released my arm and said,

"Take them off".

I reluctantly took my pants off and tossed them on the bed, Bryce grabbed my left arm and began striking me with his razor strap. Denton stood silently by our sister's bedroom door staring down the hallway trying to get a glimpse of his handiwork, for the first time he could hardly crack a smell or pretend that he was getting any pleasure, as I was beaten savagely to a pulp. I stood my ground and I didn't shed a tear or make a sound. Bryce talked and yelled at me as he feverishly struck me with his razor strap.

I could smell the stench of alcohol on his breath as the power behind the belt swiping increased with every word.

" Get your lazy butt out of the bed and go to the bathroom".

I didn't say a word. He whipped me for what seemed like an hour and all of a sudden he stopped, he looked down at me then folded his belt in his hand and back down the hallway he went. He turned to look back at me. I steadfast with a blank expression on my face displaying no tears, no pain and demonstrating no fear. I had lost all respect for him and I wasn't about to give him the joy of seeing me cry from any more of this unnecessary whippings.

I decided not to stay in my room and pout, I went down the steps and settled down on the couch. The stinging from the belt hurt beyond repair but I didn't give Denton the satisfaction of believing he accomplished his mission. I believe Denton felt bad for once about telling on me, he could see I was hurt emotionally and not physically but my spirit was nearly broken. He could see the light and excitement in my eyes was no longer there and the shift in my personality, the happiness and joy was being beaten right out of my soul. As much as he didn't like having me around him, he left me alone. He never told Bryce about the nocturnal monster again. I made my way back upstairs and lay quietly face down on my stomach.

I could still feel the sting from the razor strap. Denton came into the room and stared at me from the door. I turned my head and toward the wall. I didn't understand Denton's rationale, why did he harvest so much hate in his heart toward me, and he was supposed to be my big brother, someone who was supposed to protect me not harm me. I never understood why my mother never uttered a word about her disapproval of the uncontrolled and unnecessary beatings she allowed Bryce to give me. Maybe she believed it was necessary because she knew no other way to prevent the nocturnal monster from showing up. Denton must've felt a tremendous amount of guilt, because the next day he let me walk 10 paces behind him and his friends and never tried to ditch me throughout the day. That was the last time Denton reported to Bryce my uncontrollable bedwetting and it was the last time Bryce ever whipped me.

*C*amels hump

The summer was still young and the sun shone brilliantly through my window telling me another fun summer day was mines for 18 hours. Sherry and Marica worked all summer, they were like worker bees busy at the work, selling flower seeds and doing odd jobs around the neighborhood, such as babysitting and gardening. Two months into their hard labor they both were able to purchase brand-new bicycles fresh out-of-the-box. These were beautiful pink bicycles with streamers hanging from the handle bars and glittery pink seats. Pink fenders provided the perfect finish with a mirror on each handlebar and a reflector on the back seat.

Sherry was reluctant to let me ride her bike even though I begged and begged her. She reminded me of the time I took off on her bike in the rain then wrecking the bike before she could catch me. Marica was a little more trusting because she never had a bike and I never borrowed anything from her in the past.

"I'll let you ride my bike" she said, holding onto the handle bar.

Pointing her finger at me, she said.

"Don't go up camels hump!"

Releasing the bike, Sherry, Jenny and I took off down Park Avenue to Fairfield Boulevard, and there camels hump stood 30 feet tall, cover with the greenest grass I've ever seen with the exception of a thin dirt trail leading up the hill. Camels hump was legendary for sending kids home with scraped up knees and bent bike frames. Campbell's hump was well known throughout the neighborhood by any young person with basic bike riding ability. The hill challenged you without saying a word. Its towering presence was menacing enough. No kid ever rode past the hill without venturing up to its peak.

Jenny a skinny little girl with buck teeth and longhair, yelled out.

"Let's go up camels hump!".

I look at her nervously as she started pushing her bike up the hill. Sherry looked into my eyes, then grabbing the bike seat, she said.

"You know what Marica said, don't take her bike up camels hump".

'Jenny' " Come on Michael are you afraid?"

That's all it took and I was off pushing Marica's bike up camels hump. Jenny waited patiently until I reached the top of the hill. Being the responsible young adult she was Sherry waited at the bottom of the hill, yelling.

"I'm going to tell on you. She said, don't take her bike up there!

Down the hill Jenny went, nearly losing control of her bike, coming to a sliding stop right as she reached the street. I sat at the top of the hill that seemed 50 feet in the air.

"Holy moly"

I thought to myself. "Well, I can't stay here forever" and down the hill I went flying out of control.

The handle bars began vibrating violently as if they were going to fly right out of my hand. Suddenly, I lost control and the handle bars turned completely in the other direction. I flew off the bike tumbling three times in the air, soon I landed on the asphalt face down. While I laid on the ground in other disbelief, trying to collect myself. Jenny went back up the hill for a second run and to add insult to injury she came crashing down right on top of me.

Marica's brand-new bike appeared to be totally destroyed. The handlebars were bent totally in the opposite direction, all the air had been knocked out of the back tire. The fenders were bent and mangled up beyond recognition, the streamers were missing and the frame was scuffed up beyond repair. Sherry laughed and snorted as she rode ahead of Jenny and I. Jenny and I limped all the way back home. I could Sherry from a distance giving Marcia the bad news.

Marica grabbed her bike and went into full shock.

" I told you not to go up camels hump!" She said,

Angrily fighting back her tears. The bike was rideable I thought, it just needed new fenders and maybe a paint job. Needless to say, she never let me ride her bike again and I was reduced to being a spectator, no one trusted me to ride their bike, because I still didn't have camels hump out of my system. Although I had crash a perfectly good bike and skinned my legs to the bone, I still had another run in me.

Park Avenue was fun and exciting, and unknown to my mother I spent a lot of time walking in Fall-creek River catching goldfish and crawdads. Dwayne, Titus and I were close friends as anyone could get, but during the night they were forced in the house at 7 o'clock and would not reappear until the next morning. Denton and I would slip back outside right after my mother left for work. We walked up and down the alleys, cutting through back yards and occasionally stopping by different homes to see if our friends could come out. Although I told them Dwayne couldn't come out they decided to stop by Dwayne's house anyway. The front porch was dark and rather creepy, two eye laid near the front door glowing in the dark. The closer we got to the door growling noises intensified with every step. Because of the fear factor placed upon me by my brother I didn't back away I kept moving forward.

I couldn't stay with my brother if I showed any signs of being scared, so I went on the porch as I was expected to without showing the slightest signs of being timid.

Dwayne's mutt of a dog growled as we walked on the porch, everyone greeted his dog by saying, " Hi Champ" then jumping over the concrete divider separating the two porches. I was the last one to greet Champ.

"Hi Champ" I said forcefully, pointing my finger toward him. As I turned to walk away, Champ leaped in the air and latched onto my rear end scraping my skin with his teeth.

"Wow! I yelled grabbing onto my butt.

"What's wrong?"

Denton asked as he walked down the street.

"Nothing" I said, grabbing onto and clucking my butt.

The bite hurt for an entire week but I couldn't let anyone know that I had been bitten because I didn't want to go to the hospital again. Two months later the dog was shot by police. According to Denton, he claimed the dog had rabies. But I came to realize it was just another one of his ploys to scare me. My older brothers and sisters took great joy in scaring me, and I took great pleasure in making myself a nuisance around them and their friends every chance I got. That's why they called me Mikey.

*P*irates booty

The summer was spinning by like a driver at the Indianapolis 500 race track. We were having so much fun we didn't even notice how quickly the fall was approaching. Denton, Vernon, Johnny and I were out late one night after my mother left for work. For the first time I was able to participate in their mischievous escapades. I was overjoyed to be a part of their group and thrilled they allowed me to trail close behind, armed with my rubber band gun loaded with a bottle cap ready for action. We ran down the alley like a disorganized mob, turning over dumpsters and hurling rocks at streetlights, missing the street lights by a baseball mile. We were moving so fast I didn't notice we were 3 to 4 miles from home. The night was getting long and as scared as I was of the return of the nocturnal monster, I was ready to go home and go to bed.

The hour was approaching midnight and we decided to venture back toward familiar territory, all of the sudden Johnny took off running.

I said to myself "where is this fool going" he was running towards the bakery glass door.

I thought he would come to a screeching halt but before I knew it, he jumped right through the glass door. Glass shattered all around him hitting the ground, he slipped and slid on the fallen glass then ran inside the bakery, grabbed two loaves of bread and ran down the dimly lit street. The alarm sounded, my brother ran. I went to the bakery door in anticipation of grabbing more bread; I knew there was no point in getting the bread other than proving my worth to the bread bandits.

We all started running at a full stride, I heard sirens in the distance, my heart was beating like an African drum. For the first time I feared for my freedom. I just knew we were going to jail. Once we reached our backyard I collapsed to the ground. Johnny was laughing as he tossed his loaves of bread in the air, refusing to share his pirate's booty with anyone.

"Are you freaking retarded or what?" I said.

Trying to catch my breath.

(Johnny) "What did you say"

(Mikey) "You heard me, you fucking retard.

Johnny ran towards me so fast I didn't have time to think, so I release the clothes pin on my rubber band gun, and shot him in the eye with a bottle cap. I was as surprised as he was, I didn't even know my rubber band gun had so much power. Johnny screamed in agonizing pain and grabbed his eye. I ran into the house and observed him in pain from the back door.

Tears stream down Johnny's face as he covered his left eye swearing he would kill me when he catches me. I was quick to reload my rubber band gun and dared him to step a foot inside the house. I took my left foot and slammed the kitchen door shut, ran upstairs and listened quietly by the window with Rabbit ears; I could hear Denton and Johnny plotting against me.

(Denton) "I'll get Mikey to come out with us tomorrow night and once we are far enough away from the house I'll let you beat him up".

Johnny rubbed his eye, splashing cold water from the outside faucet on his face trying to relieve the sting of the bottle cap. He agreed to their new plot and began his painful walk home. Denton was thoroughly pissed off at me but he couldn't give his plans away so he didn't say a word.

I was up pretty early the next morning, the nocturnal monster was nowhere to be found. I was pleased with myself and I knew it would be a good day, until I sat at the kitchen table and tried to eat my overcooked cream of wheat Marica had prepared an hour earlier. She was notoriously known for her overcooked or uncooked meals, such as the raw potatoes she prepared for lunch.

There was no happy medium for her, it was well done or raw. I spent the morning with Carvale dragging a wagon down the alley and rummaging through trash cans for pop bottles. Once we collected enough bottles to fill several containers, off to the grocery store we went to collect our five cents per bottle. We wasted no time loading up on cookies, potato chips, and soda, then returned to Carvales basement and perched our feet up on top of empty boxes, reclining back against a dirty pile of clothes while we sipped down Nehi-high grape soda and choked down packages of cookies after a hard day at work. I could see someone's shadow outside the window, there were two heads peeking in and out. It was Johnny and Denton peeking through the basement window, they began beating on the glass begging us to share our pirate's booty with them, so I stood close up on the window and slowly twisted the cookie apart, licked the icing off, then shoved the naked cookie through the dryer vent.

They went ballistic making all types of threats, but I was in sugar heaven and couldn't hear a word; Therefore, I reclined back on my pile of dirty laundry and drink my Nehi grape soda and made the chips and cookies disappear one by one. Before I knew it, the night was upon us once again. I sat on the front room floor watching a rerun of the Wizard of Oz, Denton looked at me and said.

"Come on man let's go".

I sat for a brief second pondering what I heard Denton and Johnny talking about the night before, but if I was to go with them I would surely need an advantage so I ran upstairs reached under my bed and dragged out my PF Flyers. I just knew this would give me the advantage I needed. If Johnny tried anything I could escape with the quickness. Off we went into the night to cause more destruction than the night before. As usual, I stayed behind my allowed 10 paces, but for some strange reason they signaled me to come up with the rest of the group.

Unfortunately for them I had the six sense of a wolf, I could detect what was going to happen before it happened. As they turned the corner I could see part of Johnny's shirt blowing around the edge of the building. Johnny stood at the ready waiting to pulverize me as I turned the corner. That's when my PF Flyers kicked into action. I took off like a bat out of hell, running down the alley, jumping fences and turning corners like I was on rails. I ran into the house and collapsed on the floor laughing to myself.

"They must think I'm the stupidest kid in the world" I said to myself. Congratulating myself for escaping another one of Denton's plots.

Summer had ended with a bang, capped off by the return of Denton to my grandmothers house. I started school in September entering the fourth grade. I was dressed to impress, wearing a gold silk shirt; brown pin striped pants and brown patent leather shoes that were two sizes too small. I was always known for fashion, I knew the shoes were too small but it was my first time having shoes with a buckle on the side. I had two outfits to wear for the entire year, my shoes were too small for my feet with only myself to blame. While shopping with my mother I tried on two or three pairs of shoes, they all fit my feet, but the ones I liked were too small, but I was willing to suffer the pain to have style, so I pretended the shoes fit like gloves and persuaded my mother to buy them.

To keep the circulation going in my feet I spent the next few months taking my shoes off once I reached the class room. I was growing up fast, now in the fourth grade but still at an impressionable age. It was the late 1960s and life had not yet challenged me and major life influences had yet to show its face. New friends meant new experiences; tough guys emerged from every hallway, unruly and misbehaved. As part of recess my class would go across the street to Fall Creek park for lunchtime recreation. Several classes walked to the park at the same time including one teacher from every class. I was the first to make it across the street because I wanted to be the first one to climb onto the swing sets. There was a wading pool, 2 feet deep surrounded by a 10 foot high fence. I swim in the pool many times but as I grew older the pool became too shallow for my aquatic needs. The teachers were still directing the other kids across the street so this gave myself and my other classmates plenty of time to explore behind the swimming pool and make our way down to the river.

T he beehive

Every day at 12 o'clock the class was released and escorted across the street to fall Creek Park. The park was very outdated with a limited amount of recreational equipment. There were two sets of swings, a basketball court and a 2 foot deep pool for kids eight years old and under. A group of 13 boys and I went behind the swimming pool building, where we found a large Beehive. Our teacher warned us to come from behind the building and to leave the bee hive alone. All the boys slowly moved from behind the pool wall, except Michael Jones, showing that he could rebel against authority, and trying to prove how defiant he was. Michael's brothers had reputations for winning fights, but the talent for fighting was not passed down to Michael.

Michael was not tough but this did not stop him from living off his brother's reputation for fighting. One afternoon Michael wanted to prove how tough and defiant he was. Once the teacher was preoccupied with the other kids, Michael Jones took a long stick and jammed it right up the middle of the bee hive. The bees went crazy, swarming wildly trying to protect their queen. Forcing everyone back. Michael was trapped, unable to go in any direction and all of a sudden the hive fell straight down on top of his head. He yelled and screamed in agonizing pain, rolling around on the ground unable to escape the beehive trapped under his body, as he rolled around the beehive rolled around with him. I never saw Michael again. I only heard rumors that he was walking on his toes from that day forward.

Our school had its share of good and bad teachers. One teacher in particular I will never forget is Mr. Schmidt, an unselfish and giving person. These were times where the American color line was drawn in the sand and the twisted face of hate was the mask of the day. The only time a black person got invited into a white person's home was to serve food or clean the house. Sometimes I think Mr. Schmidt did not see the color line or he just ignored it.

On Halloween 1969, Mr. Schmidt, orchestrated a way to take the entire class trick or treating, and during Christmas he invited the entered class to his home, took us caroling door to door and gave each student a Christmas gift. Mr. Schmidt found creative ways to get kids to learn subjects that were not interesting. He did more than his job required and that's what teaching is all about, loving what you do. I learned to see America from a different perspective; this is the second time in my young African American life that someone of a race other than my own showed me kindness, and unselfish love without expecting reciprocity or quid pro quo. Mr. Schmidt kindness and unselfishness was short lived but not forgotten. Over the course of five years my mother had been working double shifts late into the early mornings, and with a little patience and focus, she was able to put away enough money for a down payment on a new home. We soon were moving again but this time into our own house.

2 9Th and Talbott

My mother's diligence was now paying off. Working early mornings and late nights' finally paved the way for a new future. Owning a new home was not without its envious neighbors and family members. We had the newest house in a four-mile radius, and my mother looked the world in the eye, took its best punches and came out smelling like roses. The house was filled with new furniture in every room, one TV in each room and a new car. People no longer looked at my mother in sorrow, but in confusion, they wanted to know how one young woman with eight children and apparently no husband or child support could buy so many new things all by herself. Everyone had something to say, the closer the people were to us, the more negative comments we had to hear. How they thought she was going to fail or lose her new car or her new house. What most of these people didn't know is my mother is a survivor. The kind of survivor that draws from inner strength, the same inner strength that my grandfather had when he raised six girls on dead end jobs that broke his back eight hours a day. This strength moves through the blood of our entire family. Some family members are aware of this gift and some ignore it as though it's the plague.

Moving to 29th and Talbot Street was a big project for my family. Denton and I was in charge of moving the trash barrel from the old house to the new house, because in the early 70's we burned our trash every night between the hours of 6pm and 7pm. Trash pickup didn't come along until 1973 where every house would buy two alumina trash cans. Most trash cans did not last more than three months at any given time, due to the throwing, slamming and mishandling of the cans. Using the cans for basketball practice didn't help either.

29th and Talbot was a street that welcomed characters. The names alone would scare the average person. Googie, Nene, Nibbles, Cookie, Hippy, Bede, Pewee, pookah, bey,bey. Uncommon names for an uncommon neighborhood. The neighborhood was jam packed with kids, every house had at least five or more kids in the family. The entire block came together over the years and merged into one big family. I made friends fast; the girl next door named Angela thought I was handsome, she openly demonstrated her affection for me by giving me her older sister's fresh out of the box leather baseball glove.

The glove was new and made to fit a left hand person, which in my case the glove was a perfect fit. Only one day had passed before her older sister Myra saw me in my front yard tossing a ball in the air.

"Hey little boy" she said, "Where did you get that glove?

"Angela gave it to me" I said.

While I tossed the ball in the air, monstrousMyra ran down the stairs in her bathrobe, the rope flung open exposing her monstrous breast. My eyes went temporarily out of focus and before I could regain consciousness from the site of nudity, she repossessed the glove right off my hand before I knew it. Needless to say Angela was embarrassed, but this did not stop her advances. Candy, kisses and unregulated wrestling matches pursued. She made me wrestle her for candy, but not without a small price. As long as I let her hands, Rome free I could have all the candy I could eat. I was too shy to agree to such a deal, so I cut my ties with her not long before she moved to another neighborhood on the West side of town.

Within a week's time I was introduced to my aging neighbors Mr. and Mrs. Jenkins. My mother had a genuine compassion for other people, mostly people that struggle and I would soon be the crusader for her passion.

" Take the lawn mower and cut Mr. Jenkins grass and don't charge them any money because they're on a fixed income". My mother said.

Of course I looked at her with a twisted face, I was dead tired. I just finished cutting our front and backyard. I pouted a little bit but I reluctantly cut their grass, just as I was finishing Mr. Jenkins slowly made his way down the concrete steps. Holding three dollars in his hand waving it in the air signaling me to come get it.

" That's okay, don't worry about it, there's no charge". I said.

Mr. Jenkins slowly made his way down the steps, then shoved three dollars in my shirt pocket. No, I said, sticking my chest out to ensure the money found its way inside my pocket.

" I can't take this" I said,

I Smiled as he turned and went back into his house leaving the three dollars hanging visibly from my pocket. My mother forcefully reminded me every time I was summonsed to cut his grass, not to take any money from him or his wife. Several months later Mr. Jenkins passed away and his wife moved into a nursing home. Within weeks a new family moved into the large three bedroom double. The family had a young girl and her two brothers. The two brothers were much older than I and their sister much younger. Puppy love was in the air, mostly on her part. Every day she would pop up at my door.

"Is Michael home?", she asked.

With a huge smile on her face.

" Mikey's in the backyard" my mother would say.

Unfortunate, for her, I was compelled by orectic thoughts of race cars and burying treasure in the back yard. I had no interest in a pugnacious young lady.

That same week Bryce's son and daughter came for the weekend. Bryce's son Gilbert decided to rummage through my mother's closet. Bryce became angry and just as I thought he was summonsed to the bedroom for some form of discipline which meant he was going to be whipped with a razor strap. Once the whipping commenced Gilbert screamed and yelled uncontrollably. I stood idling next to my mother licking the frosting off of the egg beaters she used to stir the cake. My mother paused for a second from pouring the cake batter into the pan.

"I don't like it when Bryce whips Gilbert, he whips him too hard". She said.

I froze, my eye bugged out with astonishment I couldn't believe what I was hearing. As much as I loved cake batter I couldn't even taste the batter anymore, I looked at her out of the corner of my eyes with distention. All of these years Bryce has been beating the skin off of me and she never batted an eye. So I drop the egg beaters in the sink, still dripping with cake mix, the taste had left my mouth and so did my sensibility, so I ventured down to the one place I could get it out of my system. The 29th St. basketball court where I would spend most of my youth, from the age of 10 to the age of 18 years old.

The swimming lesson

I spent my summers secretly writing notes, placing the notes in jars then adding a few cents to the jar, then I buried the jars all over the backyard. I was ahead of my time, I was creating time capsules and writing down history as if I was a historian. My mother could sense my boredom and thought it would be a good idea to sign my sisters and myself up for swimming lessons at Riverside Park. My mother, Sherry, Tiana, and Marcia went to swim lessons in the evening. Denise and I would catch the bus two days a week for three weeks until the end of our lessons. Denise was separated into a different class than I and for some reason I didn't see her until the end of the swimming lessons. I was the only male in my class and found it very uncomfortable when I had to assist a young girl with her lessons. Sometimes we were required to partner up, to help another student with their back float exercise.

The young girl was required to wrap her legs around my waist as she lay back in the water. There was one small problem. No one told the young girl to shave her pelvic area before putting on her swimming suit. The other problem was her swimming top was to big and once she swim from one end of the pool to the other, her top fell off, displaying her well proportion young virgin breasts. I was caught totally off guard and nearly drowned in 12 feet of water when her breast were exposed and her Bikini top floated past my head.

Denise and I spent the next three weeks catching the bus to and from Riverside Park. After our last day of swimming we decided to celebrate and use the bus money to buy ice cream and walk the two miles home. Being the genius I was, the 2 miles turned into 4 miles. Somehow I got off course and we ended up near Crown Hill Cemetery. I was proud of Denise, she was only seven years old but she showed true heart and endurance and sacrifice for 10 minutes worth of ice cream pleasure. As we approached the house my mother and sister's were standing on the pouch.

'Their they are" Sherry shouted!

Denise walked next to me dragging her towel, saturated in sweat with total exhaustion all over her face.

Quietly I cruised up to my room. I didn't want to be disturbed but the young girl next-door stopped by to see me. I didn't have time for girlfriends. She wanted a boyfriend, I wanted to ride bikes and play with hot wheel cars. I asked for hot wheels cars for Christmas but I got Johnny lightning cars instead.

It really didn't matter, either way I was having fun playing with my cars. Tina's brother Dennis was a heavy set kid who loved to wrestle, he reminded me of a young man from my childhood named Budgie. He was obese and slow, I could run circles around him anytime I wanted. One day I found myself in a wrestling match with him on a big grass lot across the street from our house. I could whip around his legs and get away from him easily, but once he fell on top of me, I cried wolf, making him lift his 155 pound body off of my back. Over and over and over again I cried wolf once he pinned me to the ground.

Once he got up I jumped on his back and climbed onto his shoulders, he flipped me to the ground like a rag doll, forcing my legs down and holding me to the ground. Suddenly there was a sharp cut, I screamed and yelled.

" Get up! Get up! Get off of me it's my knee, somethings in my knee" I said.

 Screaming and trying to kick. But he wouldn't get up because of my prior attempts at crying wolf. Finally I was able to get him off of my back, blood streamed down my leg as I gripped and squeezed my knee. Barley able to walk I collapsed on the front porch.

I reached down and pulled a huge piece of broken bottle from my knee. My skin was cut back so far I could see the white meat of my kneecap. I sat on the staircase inside the house clutching my knee. Bryce walked in reeking of alcohol. He staggered right past me to the stove, removed his food from the oven and began porking out on his fired pork chops and mustard greens. Leaving his plate on the table he staggered right passed me, up the steps then plopped down on the bed. He was asleep before his head hit the pillow. The next morning my mother looked at my knee, and was thoroughly disgusted that Bryce did not take me to the hospital. My knee healed with very little medical attention but left a U shaped scar for good luck.

My hair had grown, and so did my popularity. My afro had grown past my shoulders. I had grown at least another foot and I very closely resembled Michael Jackson. My new friends Chris, Enron, Victor, Lundy and Johar didn't think I looked like Michael Jackson. The band down the street thought I looked like him, so they put me up front and center on the microphone. I couldn't sing a note, but I looked the part. Enron and Piear were also in the band, although I couldn't carry a note. Enron and I grow into good fiends because of our participation in the band. Chris and I grow into good friends because we both liked to work on projects, walking in the river or playing basketball.

For some reason Chris was smaller but always better at basketball than I. Victor and I became good friends because of our mischievous ways. We often responded to life on a day-to-day basis, never planning or preparing, we just acted on our misguided behaviors and impulses. Victor and I would walk around the surroundings neighborhoods looking for mischief; we often founded it not far from our front door. I spent most of my evenings that summer rehearsing the new Jackson Five songs so I could be ready for band practice. I thought for sure that I was famous and had to do something to improve my appearance for my fans. So I decided to blow out my hair so I could increase the size of my Afro. For some reason, young girls found large Afros very attractive and I didn't want to disappoint them.

I was busy one evening blowing out my hair, trying to please the one or two fans I had who screamed my name every time they saw me. I grabbed a huge jar of crown royal grease. With the fire from the gas stove on high I placed the straightening comb directly on the burner. I was just repeating what I saw my mother do to my sisters hair a thousand times. I applied little grease to my scalp, wipe the straightening comb with tissue paper, then ran the straightening comb through my hair. I was just about done, more than halfway finished blowing out my hair. All of a sudden there was a spark, the more I fanned the spark, the more the flames spread. I fell out of the bathroom into the kitchen, my hair burning wildly out of control. Denton and Sherry jumped to their feet, slapping vigorously at my hair, but the fire continued to spread. Suddenly Sherry got the bright idea of grabbing the dish sprayer and soaking my grease filled head with water.

The flames instantly shot to the ceiling of the kitchen. I ran into the front room blinded by flames, all I could see was darkness, as if I was lost in the middle of space. The fire was finally subdued with a damped towel. I walked around in a daze with the straightening comb melted into my forehead. Denton slapped the comb from my forehead ripping off a layer of skin from my forehead, displaying 6 inches of white meat. I was barely conscious walking into the ambulance. A crowd began gathering outside, coming from the small two block radius of our neighborhood.

Everyone knew it was me, there no escaping, because I was paraded from the house into the ambulance, with my hair burnt to the root. The ambulance siren screamed, car's pulling to one side of the road. Once at the hospital I was placed onto a gurney and wheeled down the hallways familiar to my childhood. My mother got word that I would be arriving at her hospital any minute covered with third degree burns. The elevators were too slow, so she ran four flights down to triage where I was once again being held captive by people in white coats.

I was all but shook up, it was a comfort to see my grandmother, my uncle George, and auntie Dorothy in the waiting area. To my very surprise my father was there as well. He gave me hard discerning looks.

" You think its my fault don't you" he said to my mother.

"How the hell is it your fault Raymond, you weren't even there". She said.

I sat quietly in the backseat of my father's car hoping the crowd in front of my house was gone. I lay in the bed that night with a fan blowing on my fingers trying to cool the first degree burns covering both my hands.

Denton acquired burns also on his hands and arms and for the first time I was actually glad he was home for the summer. This little incident gave me a short-lived vacation, I stayed out of school for two weeks staring out the window at the kids walking to school. While at home my mother removed the mummy like bandage from my head and cleaned the burned hair from my scalp, I was then escorted to the barbershop. I sat in the chair horrified at my reflection in the mirror. My hair was burned completely down to my scalp. I couldn't help but to cry, I looked like buckwheat. But the barber was an expert, he meticulously cut and styled my hair into a crewcut fashion I've never had before, although I was keen to long hair, my short haircut was very fitting. Teachers told me I looked like a young gentleman and they like the short hair much better than the long, out-of-control Afro.

I returned home later that evening. I tried sneaking in the front door only to find my brother and his new girlfriend sitting in the red chair next to the door totally engrossed in kissing.

Being Mikey, it was my duty to watch them kiss for what seemed like an hour but was only fifteen minutes before I decided to move in for a closer look. Denton was quick to kick me in the leg, then covering their display of affection with a coat. This sexual display went on for more than a month. Whenever I heard noise and smelled strange scents coming from under the coat they used to cover themselves I would pull the coat off both of them, catching my brother's hands deep down inside his girlfriend's pants. Violence erupted soon after my twenty-five cent peep show. Denton would hit me with his hand covered with secretions, leaving residue on my back and arm. Fortunate for him our mother worked nights, and my stepfather was on the avenue drinking himself into a euphoric state of being. We didn't expect him home for at least five more hours. Bryce, my stepfather was a quiet drunk; he never caused problems or made any ruckus, he was a local truck driver, only leaving the city for special deliveries.

Bryce never gave me advice on life, never forced me to do homework, and never took me out to ball games or showed interest in me other than disciplinary action. Bryce spent his after work hours on the avenue, a place where alcoholics hang out to drink and talk loud about achieving nothing. Every other Friday, Bryce fancied himself the big spender at the bars on Indiana Avenue, It was payday and he was the host for the night, buying everyone drinks, bragging about the new house he lived in, the new car he drove, failing to mention the long hours my mother worked to buy the house and car.

Bryce lived the good life, living in my mother's house rent and bill free, nice clothes, cars, and no responsibility other than to himself and his drinking buddies on Indiana Avenue. My mother was doing financially ok, she maintained and provided for eight children. These were frustrating and difficult times, seeing my mother struggle as so many young mothers do to this day because the fathers lack the where with all to support their children.

Not only was he lacking in the financial area, but also in the area of parenting. I can't recall any special moments between Bryce and I, except once he took time to hand me a towel after I had been in a fight with the kid next door. Although he was not my father I felt that he had a responsibility as a black man to form some kind of kinship with me to ensure that I understood the world around me. The advice and direction I should have gotten, he neglected his duty and left me to experience those growing pains on my own. I was starving for attention and exposure to life. Just a few minutes a week could have made all the difference in my life. Another school year was beginning, there was rumors that the Boy Scouts were coming to our school to recruit. I was so excited I ran all the way to our school just to grab a sign-up sheet. I dreamed about being a Boy Scout my entire childhood. I would've loved to have the chance to wear those green shorts and green and Red socks with a scarf around my neck. I ran home excited holding the sign-up sheet high in the air fluttering in the wind. I busted through the door with tears of excitement in my eyes and placed the paper square only kitchen table in front of my mother. She looked at the paper over.

$20, I don't have $20 for this stuff. She said

Well, you don't need the money right now I just need the papers sign and returned. The meeting will be held tomorrow at 7 o'clock in the evening I said.

'Mother' I'm too tired I can't go to any meeting.

The next night I grab my signing sheet and ran to the meeting nonstop. The room was filled with kid and their parents. I believe I was the only kid in the crowd good didn't have a guardian with me. I listen while they lectured for an hour after which time we lined up to turn in our sign-up sheets. I smiled probably as I approach the table handing them my sign-up sheet.

I'm sorry little boy you must have your parents with you, the lady said.

I was totally devastated, I took my sign-up sheet and headed back down the dark winding Pennsylvania Street. The blackness engulf every turn of the street as my rejection from the Boy Scouts felt absolute.

I had just survived another summer on 29th and Talbot. New neighbors moved in next door, three boys and two girls.

One of the boys was in the same grade as I and I thought it was nice having a neighbor so close in age and in the same classroom. However; this kid turned out to be a total idiot. It wasn't long before his true behavior and personality came full circle. He spent most of his time starting fights on the playground during recess. During the time everyone else wanted to play, Larry was in the middle of fights at least twice a week. He quickly became a menace to everyone in the class, with the exception of a few boys who had older brothers that were recognized as neighborhood bullies.

These types of boys were high school dropouts who enjoyed hanging around the grade schools when school was out for the day. They bullied anyone smaller than themselves or larger than their brother or sister, enabling their brother or sister to remain the alpha male in school. That was one boundary Larry would not cross. Although, Larry had an older brother, his older brother didn't involve himself in gangs, therefore; Larry had no one to lean on for help. One night during one of the rare occasions when my brothers were both home and sleeping in the same room with me, we had a conversation about women, what women liked and what women wanted. Rayford was the narrator, demonstrating his voyager capabilities, telling us about his legendary sexual escapades and how many women he reeled into his cob web of decent.

$\mathcal{T}$he fight plan

Rayford had a revelation and thought it would be a good idea to show Denton and my-self what a real man looked like when he was erect. So Rayford removed the sheets and pulled out his phallic and began slowly stroking it as he described what it felt like to have sex, Denton was in awe, he leaned over the top of the bed, squinted his eyes try-ing to get a better view. I was thoroughly disgusted. I reached behind the bed, grabbed one of my shoes and threw it across the room striking Rayford on his penis, he grabbed his phallic and turned on his side.

'Rayford' "If Mikey throws another shoe I won't show you anymore".

Denton reached down from the top bunk bed and stuck his hand out to prevent me from throwing another shoe. Rayford went on stroking his phallic while Denton stared admiringly squinting his eyes in envy trying to get a clear vision. I couldn't take it any-more so I grabbed another shoe and hurled it across the room striking Rayford's phallic once again.

"Rayford, I'm not going to show you anymore thanks to Mikey",

Denton was thoroughly pissed off at my interrupting his sex education.

"Denton, "I'm going to tell Larry that you said you can beat him".

I knew for sure that I was in serious trouble, our school administrators appeared to have very little control over classroom and playground activities. Every time I looked out the window and saw a fight Larry was in the middle of it. Larry was not a big kid, but he was incorrigible. He had a house full of brothers. Even his sister looked very masculine. He was surely a troublemaker, the rumors of his fighting escapades were growing and no one was off-limits including me. Later that night I couldn't sleep. I tossed and turn the whole night imagining myself fighting Larry in front of a group of kids on the playground. I knew that Larry was a much stronger kid and had more confidence in the arena of fighting; I didn't know what I was going to do. I stood anxiously staring out the window until the sun light peeked over the top of the east-side of the Morrett hotel.

I gathered my shoes and clothes as quickly as I could then scurried down the steps to the front door, dashing past Larry's house as fast as my legs could carry me. I made it to the top of the hill of 33rd and Pennsylvania. Surprisingly, Larry stepped from behind the bushes as though he had been waiting there all along. He slowly approached me with a menacing look.

'Larry' "Your brother told me what you said; when we get to school I'm going to kick your ass on the way to the Tabernacle Church for Bible study."

For some reason I wasn't too afraid, but I also knew that I cannot win a fight against this kid, therefore; I was very conscious of his where abouts throughout the morning.

This was one of the few times during that year that we did have a teacher. Little good did that do, seeing how she was overweight, short, old, and slow. I was like a Klingon that morning. I followed close behind her throughout the morning never more than 3 feet from her at any time. When she went to the chalkboard I went to the chalkboard, when she went to the back of the classroom, I went to the back of the classroom. Larry stood in the background staring at me making faces and slapping his fist into the palm of his hand, and making impressions on his eye with his fist, then pointed his finger at me. I still wasn't overly terrified at the thought of fighting him I just didn't want to get beaten up. The teacher lined us up in the hallway as though we were having a fire drill and out the door to 34th and Pennsylvania Street.

Larry was walking one step behind me, I could fill his breath on the back of my neck, once outside I sprinted ahead of the class towards the teacher, but she was too far ahead, therefore; I stayed 15 to 20 feet behind her. I could see Larry out of the left corner of my peripheral vision walking fast, then turning into a slow jog. All the sudden he burst out into a full stride running right past me, I didn't understand, suddenly Kenny fell into the street clutching his left eye with Larry standing over him looking as if he had seen a ghost.

'Larry' "Oh I'm sorry man!" Larry exclaimed, "I meant to hit Michael not you".

Kenny continued to lie on the ground clutching his left eye, tears rolled between his fingers as he was trying not to let anyone see him cry, yes it was true, Larry had hit the wrong guy and he would have to pay for it.

The mixup was an easy mistake, Kenny and I both had big Afro's and were about the same height. From behind no one could to tell the difference between us and certainly on this day Larry definitely made the mistake of his life. Kenny wasn't in any way a tough guy, as a matter of fact he was a real wimp but he had brothers that were tough guys and notoriously known as gangsters. Once again I was protected by my guardian angels and for the second time Denton had failed miserably at his plans for having me beaten up. We continued our journey to the tabernacle church, once inside Kenny demanded that Larry sat next to him. Each time the teacher would turn her back and write on the chalkboard, Kenny would punch Larry in the jaw.

Larry was too afraid of Kenny's brothers and wouldn't think about striking back because of the ramifications. The Bible study class continued on for 45 minutes and Larry got 45 minutes of consistent right jabs to the jaw. Larry pleaded with Kenny as he confessed.

'Larry' I meant to hit Michael not you; I'm going to fight Michael on the way back to school"

'Kenny' "You better not touch Michael".

At this time I was safe and I had full control of the rest of my day. I sat back and smiled and occasionally asked the teacher to write Scripture on the board making the teacher turn her back to us and allowing Kenny to continue to pulverize Larry.

I did my part to ensure that Larry would get beaten half to death by his nemesis. I must have raised my hand 30 times that day, more times than I've ever done in two school years combined. I was the kid with all the questions that day and I kept the teacher facing the board writing down scriptures, as Larry got pulverized for the first time and the shoe was placed on the other foot. After Bible class we headed down 34th street towards the school, Larry slowly approached me from behind, this time I was fully aware of his presence, but he was not there to pursue a fight he was there to strike a deal.

'Larry' "I know how you can get out of me beating you up,"

'Mikey' "How?"

'Larry' "Buy me some Now & Laters."

'Mikey' "Kenny said, ' You better not touch me, so I'm not buying you anything".

I laughed and ran down the street to the head of the classroom. As I walked next to the teacher smiling from ear to ear, untouched and unscathed. Kenny continued to punch Larry in the face as we walked down 34th St. Once we were back in our assigned seats Larry was sitting on my right and Kenny sat directly behind Larry. I continued my discord, I was more than happy to change seats with Kenny. I smirked as I got up and moved to the seat directly behind Larry. For the rest of the day, Kenny continued to beat Larry while our teacher fell vastly asleep behind her desk. She didn't assume responsibility as teachers should do, for averting rancor between Kenny and Larry.

There was no need for Larry to fight Kenny after school because the fight would have been one-sided. Although Larry could have stomped Kenny's lights out with one hand tied behind his back he knew he would have to suffer the consequences of Kenny's brothers beating him up down the road, therefore he elected to take his beating privately in front of a few students rather than in front of the entire school. This small incident must have taken the fight out of Larry, because I never heard of him fighting again and every day at lunch time I was free to gaze out the window and witness normal play activity on the playground.

There was no more fighting because the charlatan had been shamed in front of 30 students, 'so I thought'. Larry was determined to fight me but he knew the consequences of his actions so he kept his distance and diabolically plotted his scheme. I noticed Larry whispering in a young girls ear. She had muscles like a bodybuilder and was well known for her fighting proweness. She had arms as big as my thighs and her thighs looked like something out of a comic book, big and muscular. She looked like a linebacker for the New York Giants.

I didn't understand why Larry would talk to such a girl because she wasn't his type. The assignation meeting with the muscle bound girl was very unsettling. My curiosity increased because Larry liked slim girls that he could control but she was ripped from head to toe, muscles coming out of every inch of her body. It didn't dawn on me until later that Larry canard a red herring story to get the pugilist well-built girl to fight me. Later that day the young girl walked past my music class, staring at me with Bette Davis eyes, pointing her finger at me and pounding her fist into the palm of her hand.

"I'm going to kick your ass after school" she said, pressing her fist in her eye.

I wasn't intimidated because she was only a girl but a very large girl with muscles as big as Hercules. The bell rang and their she was posted outside my classroom. I stepped into the hallway and stood close to the music teacher, Mr. Overby . Deb aggressively walked up so close to my face that I could smell what she had for lunch.

" I heard what you said about my mother". She said, with a disgruntle look on her face.

'Mikey' "I don't know what you're talking about"

'Deb' "I heard you called my mother a whore, I'm going to kick your ass after school".

There was no escaping the fight this time, it didn't matter what I said, she wasn't going to believe me. Throughout the day she stopped by my classroom, snatched the door open and pointed her finger at me. The word of the fight spread around the school like wild fire. Everyone was talking about it. I sat at my desk that afternoon staring at the clock. The clock was moving so fast I thought it was on crack. The bell sounded exactly at 3 o'clock, a huge crowd began forming outside in the usual place. After the twins stabbed Lala Johnson in the head I never watched another after school fight, I just walked away and pretended it didn't happen. But I wasn't walking away from this fight. For the first time I was the center of attention. I felt like I was standing in the middle of a crowded room screaming and no one cared to listen.

The atmosphere was full of so much excitement, you would have thought people pur-chased tickets to a heavyweight championship fight. Things looked very bleak, my nemesis was at her peak performance, she even motivated the crowd by doing several push-ups. I was in deep trouble, headed down shit creek without a paddle, so I slipped down the sidewalk and passed the crowd.

I reached the top of the 31st & Pennsylvania St.

"Thank God I was out of sight of the crowd" I said to myself.

I was one block from home and a block away from the school. I was home free for the moment until Delvon yelled out.

"Hey Michael!" "There he is right there. Hold on man where you going"?

He ran down the street and stood in front of me simultaneously stretching his hands out preventing me from going any farther. Soon the crowd caught up with us. More than 50 kids surrounded me.

The crowd parted like the red sea, Deb walked down the middle of the crowd stopping nose to nose, face-to-face. Deb began yelling and screaming but never hitting or touching me. In a minute's time Larry shoved her violently into me. I fell on the ground and she fell on top of me. She began yelling and screaming and hitting me all at the same time. I turned over onto my stomach and began laughing at her lightweight punches which anger her more. She screamed and yelled pounding me on my back. The coup de grace came when she hit me on the back of the head causing my head to hit the concrete.

Enron, yelled out. "Here you go Mikey!"

Tossing me his large Afro pick with 6 inch metal teeth. I recklessly swung the comb over my shoulders striking Deb across the face. She screamed and hollered as I threw her off my back. Jumping to my feet I hit her two more times in the face with the metal afro pick. She screamed and grabbed her face then took off running down the street. Everyone laughed and patted me on my back and I couldn't have felt any lower.

Someone yelled out.

"She has a butcher knife!"

I took off running home, once again hopping the fence and escaping into the house. The atmosphere was very tense in school the next day, there was a rumor that she wanted to fight again. I had prima facie evidence that was Larry was spreading rumors about a rematch fight. Once again after school the crowds began brewing out in front of the school. I wanted no part of it, so I slipped out the side door entrance and took the long way home, down Meridian Street. I took this route home for the next several days to avoid any conflict and within a week's time the temperament of her wanting to fight again faded away. The fight was contrived by a vicious lie spawned by Larry. But as fate would have it he was no longer the king of the playground fights. He had succumbed to being internecine with the female population of the school.

Since he couldn't victimize the young boys anymore he started picking on the girls, any girl that he liked and didn't reciprocate his feelings, he picked a fight with them. Larry began dating Anita, a girl that complemented his personality , her bellicose personality seem to fit his persona, always being called down to the principal's office for behavioral problems. She wasn't really a bad girl. I recalled the time I went to the laundromat with her and her family. I spent eight hours washing and drying clothes just to get a sliver of ice cream. She wasn't a bad girl at all, she wanted to fit in because of her low self-esteem and her need to be liked.

 Larry talked Anita into picking a fight with Patrina, a tall beautiful seemingly religious girl who didn't have an enemy in the world. Out of the blue Anita walks over and punches Patrina in the face. Larry quickly got involved, hitting Patrina so hard she fell lifelessly to the floor, only to be stomped and kicked by Larry and Anita. As she lay there lifeless on the floor, the class began to gether around as though they were seeing some type of carnival act, no one cared about the poor girl laying on the ground getting stomped half to death, and I didn't have the courage or strength to help her. After three minutes of fighting the teacher from the class next-door finally recognized that there was a fight due to all the commotion taking place in our classroom. She came in the class and abruptly ended the fight and escorted Patrina down to the nurses office.

This type of incident could be attributed to the poor supervision of our class as well as the school districts. Once again we were without a teacher, without supervision, our principal at the time would come up to the classroom, start us on an assignment then disappearing back into the quiet cavity of his office. Our class would go unsupervised for weeks at a time, sometimes we would have a teacher for a few days, but we could go for three or four weeks at a time without having a teacher. This was one of those times that allowed for the bad behavior of Larry to come unleashed, almost snuffing out the life of one of our fellow classmates.

Larry shifted his focus when another new family moved on the block, a single mother with two kids and a boyfriend. They occupied the other side of the double that Victor and Chris lived in. I didn't pay the couple much attention because their children were much younger than I. Her boyfriend appeared to be strange, I thought so anyway. Every time I went to visit Victor and Chris he stared at me glaringly as if I was a woman. He had a strange name, they called him Fuzzy Pants.

A tall, slim man pretending to know martial arts, which gave him ample opportunity to fondle little boys. Larry and his brother grew very comfortable with the hospitality Fuzzy Pants offered them. Fuzzy Pants often had them at his house spending nights and doing minor chores around the house. One day as we were all sitting on the front porch, yelling and screaming begin echoing from the window.

" You're a Fag Fuzzy!".

His girlfriend was reading one of his love letters from another man out loud.

'Fuzzy' "wait a minute Baby, it's not as it appears'.

"No Fuzzy, you're a fag! You're a fagg Fuzzy!" she said, yelling and screaming with a 32 caliber snub nose pistol in her hand.

We sat on the porch laughing and It certainly validated what I believed all along. Fuzzy Pants was gay. The lady packed her kids and her belongings and left Fuzzy to himself. Larry and his brother took comfort in having Fuzzy pants all to themselves. Spending nights and curling up on the couch together. Larry in the back, Fuzzy pants in the middle, and Larry's little brother in the front. Fuzzy pants moved out of the neighborhood as quickly as he arrived, before the neighborhood thugs found out he was a child molester as he would have for surly lost his life or been beaten within an inch of his life.

Before the month was out there was a new kid in town occupying the recently vacant space on the other side of Victor and Chris house. Johar and his family moved in. He was a little light skinned wimpy kid. He loved acting tough based on his brother's reputation. His brother was a heavyset Bible thumping tough guy until he met the real thugs of 29th & Talbot Street. Johar often got into trouble, getting into fights with much younger kids, and letting his hands get light, meaning he loved to steal, such as the time he stole a handful of valve stem caps off several Indianapolis 500 drag racing cars. Most of his time was spent picking fights in school with anyone he thought he could bully. One day he picked a fight with the wrong kid. The kid was a little wimp but he had bodybuilding brothers to back him up in case of a fight.

Johar's brother, Bunny Rabbit was a high school dropout. I couldn't help notice he was pacing back and forth, up-and-down the Grade school sidewalk,'

What's wrong bunny, why are you hanging outside this school?" I said.

(Bunny) " See that little kid over there, I'm going to beat him up."

"Who? I asked, "That little boy with the black leather jacket".

Bunny, "He beat up Johar and now I'm going to beat him up".

"You're not for real, that boy couldn't be more than in the fourth Grade" I said,

"Well that's too bad, he shouldn't have messed with my brother" Bunny said.

I noticed from a distance a well-known thug in the neighborhood crossing the street. He was the little boys oldest brother. The thug spent most of his free time with his other brother lifting weights, acting tough, and chasing girls. He walked right up to Bunny.

"What's going on man?" he said, looking at Bunny out of the side of his eye.

Bunny was so excited about fighting the little boy that he didn't hesitate sharing his plans. As Bunny talked, the body building thug began removing his belt and wrapping it around his hand, only exposing the huge cowboy buckle.

"See that little boy over there, I'm going to beat him up. Do you want help me?" Bunny said.

The thug looked at Bunny Rabbit out of the corner of his eyes, he took one step back, and yelled,

"No motherfucker that's my brother!" simultaneously beating Bunny in the face with his buckle.

The belt buckle swinging thug chased Bunny back down Pennsylvania Street only stopping a block from his home. Bunny Rabbit never hung out at the school again and never respond to Johar's cries for help. That fight would come full circle one week later, when the news filtered through our neighborhood that a local thug from one street over beat up one of the guys from our block. The word got back to the king of thugs, the alpha male, named Bey, he lived three doors down from me. He was the first and only person I had ever known to own a pet monkey. He named all his pets Sam. Bey found it distasteful that a member of our block was beaten up by a member of another block.

It wasn't long before Bunny Rabbit saw the belt swinging thug hanging out on 30th and Central. "Look he said, there the motherfucker goes right there. Bey casually strolled over as though he was going into the liquor store and before anyone knew it Bey punched the belt swinging thug in the mouth. To my surprise the belt swinging thug ran off into the night he didn't even try to fight back. Bunny Rabbit stood idly by smiling from ear to ear as the belt swinging ran off. The thug ran for help two blocks over and returned with four friends several minutes later. They came around the corner walking at an infantry's pace. I just knew there would be blood shed at hand. This was just like in the movies I thought, just like West Side Story.

Bey, Rayford and two of their other friends were strolling down the street, when the belt swinging thug and his friend blocked the sidewalk, preventing Bey and his group of friends from moving any farther. One of the friends of the belt swinging thug stepped forward.

"Which one of you punched my boy in his mouth"? He said, with an intimidating look on his face.

Bey stepped forward, "I did" he said, with a forceful tone.

The other thug recognized Bey immediately and cowardly stepped back and recanted his challenge.

"I just wanted to know" he said.

They walked down the street as fast as their feet could carry them. I knew the belt swinging thug and his friend from my days of living on 30th and Park Avenue. I've never known them to back down from a fight, they were normally the perpetrators of fights, but now I had a new profound disrespect for their thuggish nature.

School went on pretty much the same for the next three weeks. I didn't understand the system; I wasn't learning a thing, most of the time I sat in the back of the classroom with Jedrek Goodnite drawing pictures from the political articles that I cut out of the news paper the night before. Not paying attention to anyone or anything in the classroom, I was systematically learning how to block out education and the confrontations in the classroom by drawing the atmosphere out on paper.

I don't recall Jedrek ever doing any school work during our class session, the only activity he ever took part in was art. From the time we sat down in the morning until the time the school bell rang at 3 PM Jedrek was engaged in drawing. I didn't realize at the time he was masking the pain that he felt from the recent death of his mother who was an artist as well. I just thought he was another kid too dumb to do the work, therefore; he chose to draw instead. I was never more wrong.

A bike for Christmas

I spent most of my summer that year trying to piece together bicycles, I spent hours on the patio cleaning up and sanding down rusted out chains and searching up and down allies for bits and pieces of bike parts. I was one of the few boys on the block that didn't own a bike. I would jog behind the other kids trying to keep up with them while they rode their bike's leaving me behind at their will.

I became very discouraged with the idea of not having a bicycle of my own. One morning, Victor, Landus, Enron and I rode our bikes toward the 60th block of Meridian Street. Victor and I rode on the handlebars while scouring the neighborhood for unchained bikes. And there it was, a brand-new Orange Crate bicycle standing unlocked in the bike cage.

The owners, two eight-year-old white boys just walked in the variety store leaving their bikes free for the taking. Victor looked at me and before he could complete his sentence daring me to take the bike, I jumped off the handle bars of Landus bike. I ran down and snatched the bike from the bike cage before the seat was cold. Victor followed right behind me snatching the other bike as the two young white boys ran behind us screaming.

"Bring back my bike, Bring back my bike".

We rode off like bats out of hell, taking side streets ensuring that we didn't run into the police. Victor laughed the entire way home, I was a nervous wreck because I knew I couldn't keep the bike. So I gave it to Victor in exchange for the older disfunctioning bicycle he took from the bike cage. I knew it wouldn't be hard to explain to my mother where the older bike came from because I had been building bikes from scrap all summer but I never had enough parts to complete an entire bike. But she asked anyway.

" Where did the bike come from?" she asked.

I pretended like I was working on the bike.

"I got different parts from different people and put it together." I said, looking at her out of the side of my eye.

I felt so guilty about stealing the bikes that within the week I gave the other bike away as well. Every time I went out of the house I was a nervous wreck thinking the police could show up any minute and carry me to juvenile hall. The days I didn't spend at the basketball court I was in search of parts for building a bicycle or walking up to Douglas Park to swim or just relax by the pool. Our summer recreational options were limited. A two-week day camp was the best the city could offer.

We had a basketball court, a sand box, and a couple of horseshoe pits for our entertainment. Anyone with eyes could see that our neighborhood was economically deprived of recreational sponsoring. The city took our taxes and sent the money to the more fluent neighborhoods, allowing them to build cabins and to buy recreational equipment for their summer camps. Occasionally the Parks and Recreation Department would arrange for us to take trips to some of their day camps at Eagle Creek Park and other large parks in the surrounding city. Chris, Victor, Enron and I walked several blocks to 25th and park Avenue to the local pick up spot for day camp.

I thought the day camp idea was great but the recreational instructor was a little too aggressive. He did dangerous stunts and expected us to follow him. Such as going down a steep hill that ended in a 6ft deep marsh. The hill was so steep we could easily lose our footing and end up in the bottom of the marsh with water above our head. The recreation leader ran down the hill and I went right down behind him.

All the other boys took the safe paved road designed for humans to reach the bottom of the hill. But everywhere the recreational instructor went I followed no matter how dangerous. I don't know why I did it, I just did. After a day of going up and down hills and through marshes, we retired to our own little section of the camp where they serve box lunches stuffed with ham and cheese sandwiches, potato chips and the standard grape drink which lacked vitamins but was a refreshing beverage.

We raced up and down the hills to earn the left over grape drinks and potato chips. By the end of the day, arts and craft class was the last activity. The instructor was so impressed with my courage he secretly gave me a leather belt craft set while everyone else was weaving baskets or doing paper crafts. After summer camp ended we returned to our routine limited recreational options at our park, playing basketball or horse shoes. Victor and I couldn't stand the boredom of everyday life on the basketball court. So we ventured out of the neighborhood for a more adventurous and exciting life. Once we reached Meridian Street a line of police motor cycles as far as the eye could see were heading our direction.

"Get back on the grass!

Yelled one motor cycle officer. Then a long stretch limo with two American flags on the hood approached. The back window rolled down and Gerald Ford the US president waved at us as he passed by. We yelled and pointed at him as he cruised down the street. That was the highlight of my day until we discovered the rich was having a pool party at the Stouffer's Inn hotel directly across the street from where we were standing.

The temptation was too great to let this one pass us by. So, we ran down the alley and climbed over a fence into a neighbor's yard, where we picked off a bushel of crab apples. Climbing back over the fence we raced towards the pool party, clinging to the crab apples stuffed down our shirts. We took the long way around to the side of the hotel and lay flat on the inclined of the hill. We bit off the stems of the apples as if there were grenades then lay silently on the side of the hill out of sight of the rich and undeserving. They couldn't see us but we could see them living the high bourgeoisie lifestyle, so we began throwing crabapples in the air. People were running screaming and falling into the pool destroying their tuxedos and spilling their hundred dollar bottles of Champagne. We laughed as we threw crabapples in the air like hand grenades hitting everything that moved. Then we disappeared into the night like the bandits we were.

We ran down Meridian Street laughing to ourselves. At in instant Country western music stopped us in our tracks. I couldn't believe it, there was another party two blocks away at the Children's Museum, jammed packed with Europeans dressed up from head to toe in cowboy outfits. I thought all the whites moved out to the suburbs away from the urban communities. This time it was a country-western party.

Everyone was dressed up in country-western outfits, square dancing their little hearts out. We couldn't resist. This time we made fun of their music by dancing like the Beverly hillbillies and Porky the Pig. Victor would place his finger on the top of my head. I put my hands on my hips while sticking my tongue out and turned around in a circle. I couldn't believe it, they loved it! They invited us to come inside the fence and dance. A tall middle-aged white woman came to the fence and handed us five dollars apiece. We stuffed the money in our pockets and took off running down the street never completing our unofficial contract for dancing.

We took our new wealth and went our separate ways that night, not before stopping by the candy store and loading up for a midnight snack as we once again sat on the neighbors porch to watch the traffic lights, trying to stay awake until the lights started blinking. Once again we fell short of our midnight goal and headed home to the comfort of our beds.

 Before the end of the summer the city thought it would be a good idea to host an ice cream social, downtown at the Memorial Park. Ice cream trucks parked all around the square of the park on every corner. Their must've been at least 15 ice cream trucks parked in different locations. All the ice cream we could eat was free. I couldn't believe it, I ate more chocolate covered ice cream bars in one day than I've eaten in my entire life. We sat on the grass watching the fireworks and listening to music. I ate and ate and ate until my stomach poked beyond my belt line. My blood sugars ran high and I was drunk from all the ice cream I'd eaten. At 9 o'clock the social function ended. The long walk home would give me a chance to burn off the ice cream.

We headed down Meridian Street enjoying the scenic view as we walked home. Suddenly my stomach began to rumble and with every step I began to fart, then there was more pressure and all of a sudden I had the urgency to go take a number two. I ran ahead of the crowd, trying to make it home before I had a messy accident. My stomach wasn't letting me off the hook from eating all that ice cream. I ran and ran and ran until I was ahead of group by three blocks. I made it as far as Fall Creek Bridge, the pressure from the ice cream wasn't taking any prisoners, so I had to ditch down by the riverbank, pull down my pants and let it rip. The ice cream blow out of me like an uncorked bottle of champagne. All the ice cream I had just eaten ended up on the bottom of the river floor leaving my carbon print for the next generation to find. My summer ended with a bang and a sense of urgency, but my pipes were clean.

The beginning of school was upon us once again, but the style of dress totally changed. Bell bottoms pants, platform shoes and hot pans were the fashion of the day. I saved enough money to purchase a brand-new pair of Converse sneakers, this time a pair that fit my feet. My mother didn't purchase bell bottoms, however she did purchase two pairs of Wrangler jeans. I pressed my jeans all night trying to get ready for the first day of school. I was entering the seventh grade and had to look the part. I didn't care about my education I only cared about how I looked. My hair grew back in superb fashion, longer than It was before the fire. My mother did such a great job putting on the cocoa butter, consistently applying it to my forehead, ears and fingers, the discoloration went away and you couldn't even tell I had ever burned myself.

Winter was upon us once again, Jack Frost was serious this year, the nip of the wind was a little colder, and the temperatures fell a little farther. The coldest day of 1973 was December 22, with a low temperature of-3°F. For reference, on that day the average low temperature was 24°F and the low temperature dropped below 8°F only one day in ten. The coldest month of 1973 was January with an average daily low temperature of 23°F. I really didn't care how cold it got, a new bike could cure all the coldness Jack Frost could Manifest. However, Christmas did arrive, my brother Rayford couldn't wait for Christmas morning, so he took a gift into the bathroom, unwrapped it, played around with it, resealed it and placed it back under the tree. I was too scared to try such tom foolery. I waited patiently for the next morning.

I sat in a red chair next to the front room door trying to catch a glimpse of the huge bicycle box stuffed behind the Christmas tree. I was so excited I couldn't sleep. I sat at the top of the stairs listening to my mother and brothers assembling the bike. I practically went to bed around 7 PM trying to rush the night by, leaving the bedroom door slightly ajar just enough to see my mother and brothers busy at work taking Christmas gifts from her closet and placing them under the tree. I fell asleep with my face hanging over the edge of the bed, never seeing Santa or finished seeing the completion of my bike. Five in the morning I was already awake. I sat at the top of the staircase waiting for my mother to give the okay to go downstairs.

" Who's on the staircase!" She asked, in a loud but exhausted voice.

No one replied, I sunk back to my bedroom and my sisters went back to their room.

At 6 o'clock sharp I found myself once again sitting at the top of the staircase!

"Go on downstairs!"

My mother yelled from her room. All you could hear was eight set of feet tumbling down the staircase all at once. I rushed directly over to the bicycle, smiling from ear to ear, and to my surprise it was a girl's bike. I was flabbergasted, I didn't want to see any of the other gifts, the bike was the only thing I care about and as far as I was concerned Christmas was over at that moment.

Denise ran downstairs, jumped on her bike and rode it from the front room to the kitchen and around the kitchen table. I sat on the staircase staring at Denise's bike with a defeated look on my face, watching my brothers and sisters tear into their gifts. It appeared they got everything they asked for. Easy Bake oven's, Barbie dolls, radios, watches, a drum set for Rayford, a guitar and amplifier for Denton. My mother did a great job as a single parent, providing us with our Christmas wishes, but somehow I felt lost in the shuffle of eight children. I received only one gift that I asked for, a digital watch.

The sun came up, and for the first time all week the temperature rose up to 25°, just-warm enough for Denise to take her bike out onto the snow covered sidewalks. The streets were jam-packed, kids riding their new bikes up and down icy and snow cover ed streets. Icicles hung from the tree limbs, the sun shone brilliantly, melting the small patches of snow on the sidewalks as if it knew to clear a path for one day of excitement.

I presented a hapless figure as I leaned against the fence in envy, wishing I could've gotten a bike that year. My farouche behavior did not win me any friends that morning. Denise was cognizant of my disappointment, she graciously stopped her bike in front of me.

" Here you can ride it".

I quickly jumped on the bike taking it for spin around the block, but it wasn't the same and it wasn't my bike. I grew bored very fast riding a girls bike up-and-down the street, being laughed at by my friends. I resigned myself to the house and watched my sisters make cakes in their new Easy Bake ovens.

They put on their little aprons, pour the Jiffy cake mix into a bowl. Once the preparation was complete, they poured the mix into a little metal tray and slid it into their Easy Bake oven. They sat there for hours looking into the oven door of their Easy Bake oven watching their cake being baked by a lightbulb. Two hours when by and the cake mix was as raw as when they first put it in the Easy Bake oven.

"Could you watch my cake while I go to the bathroom". Tiana said.

"Sure I'll watch it" smiling from ear to hear.

As soon as I heard the bathroom door shut, I drank the cake mix out of the metal pan then tossed the pan back into Easy Bake oven. I love cake. I didn't care whether it was uncooked batter are completely baked, I just love the way it taste.

I grabbed my basketball and ran down the street toward the basketball courts. I could hear Tiana screaming and hollering from a half block away. I wasn't too concerned because a box of jiffy mix only costed 15. Cent. I stayed at the basketball court that afternoon freezing half to death. The temperature was no more than 29° but we didn't care because the older boys didn't come out to play basketball in the cold weather. We had the court all to ourselves. One thing that always work in my favor I had a lot of sisters which attracted a lot of girls. Every time I walked in the house it was like a concert just for women. Girls fill the front room, Cupid, Faye, Diane, Nipples, Kim, Cookie and some other girls I didn't know. I hid behind the couch as a little brother would do, and tossed my shoes at them as they walk past.

Someone suggested we should have a snow ball battle, girls against boys. We all ran outside across the street to the big empty grassy field and began making fortress for protection. Chris, Victor, Enron, Lundy and I rushed to make hundreds and hundreds of snowballs, preparing for the battle we were surely to win. Once the battle began I couldn't bring myself to hit anyone with the snowballs except for my sister Tiana. It took 30 minutes to build a fortress and the snowball battle lasted just as long. The sun began to set, the cold air developed more of a nip with the disappearing of the sun. My tennis shoes were soaking wet and my toes were frozen like french fries. My fingers were frozen in place and I could no longer make a snowball or attempt to throw one.

One by one everyone disappeared into their homes leaving our fortress in place. The snowball battle ensued is everyone went about the way throwing snowballs at each other as they went toward their front door. These were cold but good times, times that we would never relive again. The next morning I searched my pockets for loose change but all I could find was lent filling the crevices in my pocket. Snow was falling by the tone and all of a sudden I had a bright idea.

I grab my shovel, walking house to house charging three dollars a yard to shovel their sidewalk. I worked until I had enough money to purchase a half pint of ice cream, a pack of cookies and a soda. The thought of those refreshments motivate me to walk from house to house until someone trusted me to shovel their sidewalk properly. After working diligently for more than an hour I did get my first $4 and off to the 7-11 grocery store I went. I decided to take a shortcut through the parking lot of the Stouffer's in hotel. Something was amiss, there were streamers and declarations around the entry to the hotel.

A big sign with a picture of Jerry Lewis also stood at the entry way. It was the Jerry Lewis telethon. Being the mischievous, curious kid I was I ventured into the hotel. Signs lead me down the hallway and into a big room where gruff the crime dog was on television taking donations. I sat in the audience watching and cheering before deciding to donate three of my hard earned $4. Every kid that walked up got a hug any chance to be on TV before gruff took their money.

I was next in line, gruff the crime dog looked right past me, I wave my money in the air trying to get his attention but he went right to the next little white boy or girl not bothering to acknowledge my presence. So I toss the money in the donation can and walked out. I've never been so humiliated in my life I did not understand it and I wasn't going to stick around for an explanation, there were new chips coming out on the market," Doritos" .75 cents a bag and I wasted no time being the first in my family to sample the Doritos.

$\mathcal{T}$he educational leap

This school year was different, the kids in my class were much older and getting in-volved in more heinous activities. One boy brought a bottle of Wild Iris Rose wine to school. He led four of us into the bathroom. We stood around a huge metal sink sipping on the bottle of wine. I recognized the bottle from when I was eight, the time I got drunk and I could barely walk up the steps. I thought the taste was disgusting then, and I had not acquired a taste for it yet. I stuck my tongue over the whole of the bottle, moving my Adam's apple up and down pretending as though I was drinking.

The other boys drank from the bottle, belched as if they were men or of some impor-tance. Back to the classroom we went, the five of us huddled in the corner of the back of the classroom. The four boys were for surely high, I just pretended to be high so I could be a part of the tough guy group, but I didn't feel anything because I didn't drink anything. For the next two months, right before class began I was summoned to the bathroom and presented with a bottle of Wild Irish Rose.

I was the only one in the group that had some form of income. Between my brother's sexual escapades and working in the variety store I had a weekly income of around $45. But I was reluctant to financially participate in the buying of alcohol. I mostly sat in the class and watched the other boys slumping in their chairs. I was no stranger to the effects of alcohol and I refused to be a poster child or accused of being a drunken student. Soon the perpetrator that had the ability to buy the wine was discovered.

He was a young man that everyone knew, he was an alcoholic by the time he was in the eighth grade. He dropped out of school and began a life of drinking and hanging out at the 500 liquor store on 28th and central where most of the would be tough guys found themselves after there was no one else to bully. By the time the young man was 25 he was barely able to walk and soon after he died as a result of his alcoholism.

Later that morning I was escorted to the principal's office by the dean of boys. I thought for sure he found out about our unauthorized drinking in the bathroom.

"Sit here" he said.

I looked through the glass separating his office from the waiting room as he sat at his desk and fumbled with the wooden paddle. I took a deep breath and thought to myself.

"I wish I had taken a sip of the wine now, at least I wouldn't feel the paddle".

A heavyset short woman, wearing glasses with pop bottle Lenses tapped me on the shoulder, "Come this way please" she said. She handed me four pages of extremely difficult words, words I've never seen before. She asked that I put a check mark by all the words I knew.

Then she gave me a puzzle to put together while she timed me. Next she came to my home and discussed with my mother about advancing me to the ninth grade the following year.

"I have to inform you, we're considering advancing Michael to the ninth grade next year" she said.

Staring intensely at my mother while holding a clipboard.

" I don't know about that" my mother said. (mother) "What do you want to do?" Do you want to go to the eighth grade with your friends? Or do you want to go to high school?" It's your choice". Smiling, I reclined back in my chair.

" I want to go onto high school" I said.

The truth was, I just wanted a break from the people I've known since the third grade. I wanted to see a different crowd and be in a different place. I was excited for change, and couldn't wait for the opportunity to be around more mature individuals. I returned to class feeling uplifted, in truth I felt a little superior to all the seventh graders in my class. I felt more intelligent, one level above my peers. I kept it a secret to myself until the summer break I let it be known to my closest friends that I would not be returning to Mapleton Fall Creek school.

Of course they didn't believe me but the following year when school started in the month of September, I cruised right past their playground. I was proud as a peacock as I strutted past the kids encaged behind the fence. Several of the kids yelled out my name as I waved to them smiling from ear to ear. They couldn't believe I was going high school. Some of the girls were so full of admiration, I was even invited to walk one home. Every time I walked past the fence, a young girl would approach and ask that I walk her home. She was in the eighth grade and now I was in the ninth and I didn't think it appropriate that I date someone much younger than I.

But she was unrelenting. After school she would grab my hand and ask that I escort her home. I didn't see any harm and since chivalry wasn't dead I obliged her. Her name was Susan and someone taught her well about how a young man should treat her and the old traditions of walking a lady home. She stopped me in my tracks and moved me to the other side of the sidewalk.

"A man is supposed to walk closer to the street" she said.

Smiling, she wrapped her arm around mine then shoved her books in my hand. She was a beautiful girl and well mannered. Everyday was the same thing, I walked her home, then settled down to a nice quiet evening of holding hands on her front porch. Sex wasn't on her mind, but I was being coached by my friends. They advised me to break up with her if she wasn't putting out. Later that year her family moved out on 86 street and that pretty much ended our relationship for the lack of transportation on my part, and I wasn't willing to ride my bike 10 miles just to hold hands on the front porch.

A White Castle summer

Summer was beginning to feel long and drawn out. We were running out of things to do or should I say constructive things to do. Either way I was ready to return to school. Most kids were in the house by 9 o'clock including myself but I would slip back outside as soon as my mother went to work. We settled down for the night on my neighbor's front porch watching the stoplights, waiting for them to start flashing at midnight. By the time 11:30 pm rolled around my eyelids were involuntarily shutting on their own. I had no control or say in that matter so I made my way home and crawled into the bed only to be awakened by the smell of corned beef.

I know it was my older brother Rayford before I opened my eyes.

"Mikey you awoke? He said, while tapping me on the shoulder.

"I am now, what do you want" I said.

"Here's three dollars, why don't you go downstairs to sleep".

I gladly grabbed his $3 and made my way downstairs to sleep on the sectional couch. I couldn't believe it the next night he was back again, reeking of corned beef and requesting that I provide him a hotel rate of $3 to sleep downstairs. I gladly rolled out of bed snatching the three dollars from his hand while making my way to the couch.

Night after night it was the same thing, first the awful stench of corned beef smell, then three dollars shoved into my mitts. I couldn't take it anymore! The next night I stayed awake in anticipation of his arrival. He was like clock work, I heard them coming up the steps, two sets of feet pounding on the staircase, as the stench of corned beef preceded him. I squinted my eyelids pretending I was asleep, trying to sneak a peek at the well proportioned female standing next to my bed.

" I would take my clothes off but someone's in the room" she said.

"He's asleep" Rayford said.

Bending over looking in my face and tapping me on the shoulder.

" Mikey, Mikey, are you sleep". I laided still as a rock, pretending to snore.

" See, I told you he's asleep" he said.

Setting his large "20 sack bag" of White Castle Hamburgers on the table with two extra large orange sodas to wash it all down. Ahh, I thought to myself, those burgers smell refreshing. A sense of hunger and thirst rushed through my body like water through the Titanic.

The robust girl climbed under the covers and began disrobing. I squinted my eyes trying to catch a view of what a robust naked female looked like. My brother didn't waste anytime, he went right into it. I squinted my eyes and enjoyed the show. I had a young and limber body so I was able to stick my hand in the big bag of white castles, cautiously pulling out one box at a time. The burgers were still warm. The grilled onions and melted cheese made me salivate as I began porking out on a White Castle hamburger, then tossing the empty box behind the bed. The sex lasted for three minutes and for every minute Rayford was preoccupied, I ate two white castle hamburgers and washed it down with one of his extra large orange sodas. I was thoroughly fed and entertained, there was nothing else I could do but go to sleep.

After letting out a loud White Castle fart that could wake the dead, I fell into a deep sleep under my wool Flintstone blankets. The next morning Rayford was up at 6 AM sharp, rushing his latest mistake to get dressed quickly. Out the door she went before my mother arrived home at 7:30 AM.

'Rayford,' "There's White Castles in the refrigerator if you want them".

"No, I'm okay, I don't want any." I said, laughing to myself.

$\mathcal{A}$ fight among friends

The next morning I was slow getting to my feet, I was still full from the night before so I lay in bed and didn't get up for 30 minutes until the sun was slowly resting comfortably on my face. I wipe the sleep from my eyes staggering from the bed into the bathroom. I was so full from eating six White Castles that I bypassed the leftover bacon, eggs and biscuits left on the kitchen table from my mother and Bryce's breakfast. I headed straight outside down to the basketball court.

Victor and I played several games of 21 until the teenage boys used their authority, pushing us off the basketball court. We ran up and down the street and through the alleys stopping at a stack of tires, two houses from my home. Suddenly rocks begin coming from nowhere, Chris and Enron was in the garage hiding, occasionally sticking their head out and chucking rocks at Victor and I. Within seconds a full all out rock battle was in progress.

Chris and Enron had the protection of the garage, Victor and I stood in the open giving is good as we got. I glanced down looking for a rock, but the glare of a piece of broken glass caught my attention. Rocks buzzed past my head as I stood there staring at the broken bottle. The bottle was staring at me and I stared back. It was as if I was in slow motion bending over to pick the broken bottle up. Before I knew it I had it in my hand. I threw the broken bottle with the intention of making it ricochet off the garage never intending to hit anyone.

Chris began poking his head in and out of the garage as I flung the glass toward the side panel of the garage. Right as the glass was reaching the entrance of the door, Chris stuck his head out and the glass hit him in the eye. He disappeared for several seconds inside the garage and all of a sudden he came charging out of the garage with a brick in his hand. I didn't know what to do so I just took off running. I climbed up a stack of tires and fell, and before I knew it, Chris jumped on my back and smashed me in the back of my head with a brick.

I wasn't physically hurt, just my pride. So I made it to my feet and staggered into the house with blood trickling down my neck.

" What the hell happened to your hair boy?" my mother said very angrily.

"Chris hit me with the brick" I said.

Before I could tell her what happened she ran into the street and confronted Chris, then returned to the house to give me a wet cold towel to apply to the base of my head. An entire week when by before my mother allowed me to play with Chris again. I just happen to be in the backyard one day when Chris, Victor, and Enron were heading down that alley into mischief. I was bored out of my mind so I jumped the fence and joined the group. My mother yelled from the door.

"Don't come home crying if you get another brick upside he head"

I laughed and ran down the alley with my friends. Summer was a blast but it blew by as fast as it came, but not before another fight would take place between friends. Early one morning Chris and I ventured out to the basketball court at eight in morning. Just before 9 o'clock we got bored with basketball and decided to make our way down to Enron's house so we could ask him to come to the basketball court. We knocked on his door and his brother boy George answer the door.

"What do you want this early in the morning?" He said.

While wiping the morning residue from his eyes.

"Where is Enron?" Tell him it's Mikey and Chris and to meet us at the basketball court" .

Enron isn't here" said Boy George.

Then slamming the door in our face.

"You little punk, go get Enron" Chris said.

Chris continuously knocked on the front door. Boy George ran to the second floor and began throwing soap out the window at us. Chris and I begins furiously collecting the soap throwing it back at the window. Chris yelled out.

" Enron's throwing so too, I just saw him" we're going to get you Enron when you bring your punk butt out of the house".

Chris and I made our way up to street towards the children's museum. We knew Enron loved hanging out at Ray's service station, so we waited idly across the street lying on the well manicured lawn of the Children's Museum. Enron was so predictable we could had set our watches by him. Just as we predicted he came marching up the street as happy as a lark.

We jump from our hiding places and surrounded him.

"We saw you throwing the soap at us punk" said Chris.

I stood on his right side looking menacing. But Enron was my friend, I've known him since he was five years old and I was reluctant to fight him, therefore; I did the bare minimum I could have done. I shoved him making him stumble back and before I knew it Chris punched him in the stomach then we fled across the street inside the Children's Museum. Enron cried holding his stomach as he ran home. I feel horrible inside as I watch him cry his way home. I was willing to receive any punishment my parents could dish out.

Chris and I went our separate ways. Chris went to the basketball court and I was told to come home because my mother wanted speak to me. I reluctantly went home and just as I suspected my mother was going to punish me with a whipping. But fortunately for me we were on our way to our grandmothers house were visions of orange slice candy danced in front of my face in a candy dish. Chocolate cake sat three layers high on the kitchen table smother with rich chocolate icing. The smell of a three course meal and the fragrance of my grandmother's perfume came home like truth. These were the best days of my childhood, a place I always felt safe and loved.

The beauty of autumn was upon us the leaves were poetically beginning to change into beautiful orange and yellow colors as they fell lifelessly to the ground. New chores immersed as I was given the task of raking the yard and piling the leaves in a stack for burning. My little sister and our dog couldn't help but to run through the leaves creating a small mess for me to rake up.

I love the fall weather and the holidays that came with it. Holloween being my favorite, dressing up and venturing out to receive all the free candy we could eat. I was growing up but I didn't think I had out grow holloween, but due to peer pressure in the neighborhood I was thrust out of holloween by 11 years old. The neighborhood high school dropouts hide in bushes and grabbed our bags as we walk pass. This type of behavior continued and grow from bag grabbing to throwing eggs at trick-or-treaters.

I became so perplexed by the entire situation I didn't bother to dress up anymore, I just knocked on doors and stuck out my bag, but the neighbors weren't having it.

"Go home and dress up and I'll give you candy" the lady said.

I was glad she didn't recognize me from the time I threw trash in her yard and ask if I could pick it up for a quarter. These were fun times that became notorious. Running often down the street with flashlights, going door-to-door, dressed up like every creature imaginable, then the infamous bag grabbing an egg throwing began. A tradition that didn't stop until I was well out of my teens or the neighborhood thugs grew up and moved a way. The spring and the fall were my favorite times of the year. The summers were too hot and the winters were too cold, but nevertheless all four seasons arrived on time.

The holidays were upon us, I just knew this Christmas I would be riding a new bike, it was one of the gifts I had requested for the past two years. It was the beginning of another school year; the smell of fresh Blue Jeans and new clothes that were traditional for this time of year filled the air. Converses were the popular shoe of the day and every kid had to have a pair. I wasn't so fortunate, my mother was reluctant to pay $15 for a pair of tennis shoes when she was used to paying a $1. 99 for a pair of Buddy Els.

During the fall I would worked all day at Mac's candy store. He was an old nasty bald headed man who had the social graces of a Ferel cat. He was a type II diabetic with one leg. He was mean and vicious and often boasted about the days when he had both his legs. He lost his leg when a city bus hit him while he was trying to get into his car. He said the bus dragged him three blocks before coming to a stop. Mac was mean but I enjoyed being around him because he was a character.

My mother questioned the amount of time I spent around him because she saw no good coming from it. Mac candy store was pretty pathetic, the only type of candy he had for sale was boxes of chocolate Turtle candy. Turtle candy was my favorite candy in the world but even I grew tired of eating chocolate Turtle candy all day long. I sat in his store for hours watching the people walk past his window occasionally staring at the rows and rows of Turtle candy that lined the windowsill. One morning I went by the store and Mac wasn't there, he was home lying in bed in chronic pain. His leg had turned black and purple.

"What's wrong Mac" I asked, with a look of concern on my face.

He rolled back and forth in bed, moaning and groaning.

" It's my sugars boy, it's my sugars". "Handed me that medicine over yonder".

I didn't know what he was talking about but I reached over and handed him a bottle of pain meds. The next day Mac was rushed to the hospital and he returned a month later with his second leg amputated. By this time he had moved out of Lundy's house and into the back of the candy store, I played nurse maid for his first two weeks out of the hospital. I emptied his bed pan, cooked his lunch and dinner, made his bed and emptied his trash. I did all of this at no charge, I did it because I liked his character, I thought he was funny. My true reward came when he asked me to count out pennies, quarters and silver dollars and put them into rolls. Because the rolls had to have the address of the person turning them into the bank the work became even more tedious and time-consuming.

Mac had a small fortune safely tucked away inside of 10 to 12 five gallon water jugs. I never saw so much loose change in my life. I must've spent the next two months rolling quarters, dimes and pennies in bank rolls, then labeling them with his address. It was very tedious, boring and time consuming work. After stuffing coins for nine hours a day he would pay me one dollar an hour. After working an entire week he only paided me $45 for 45 hours of work. I felt as though I was being taken advantage of, therefore; I began to relieve his cash vault of several silver dollars.

At the end of the day my shoes were stuffed with silver dollars, I walked as slow as I could to prevent the jingling of coins while departing the store. The silver dollars jingled in my socks no matter how slow I walked. But Mac was no fool, he let me go about my way. He never said I was fired, but he no longer requested that I returned to his store.

Weeks went by and I would occasionally walk by the store and wave at Mac sitting behind the counter. He sat idle in his wheelchair sucking on a piece of candy nodding his head as if to say.

"Hi".

I couldn't help but to think he was lonely, seeing how no one wanted to buy Turtles candy. The next week he waved his hand in my direction ushering me into the store." What's going on Mac?" I asked, trying not to give him any indication I was happy to be employed again.

"Could you empty my bowl for me?"

I looked at him and rolled my eyes, but I couldn't help notice that the store smelled like an unfleshed toilet and burned eggs. Once I emptied his bedpan, he gave me instructions on how to cook hamburgers using two eggs and ground beef. I had to admit it was a little refreshing having my friend back. We kicked back in the store and ate egg cheeseburgers with a side of chips and a tall orange soda.

While lying in the hospital Mac had plenty of time to think, time enough to have an epiphany. He summoned a young man from down the street to drive us to the South-side of town to the candy warehouse. I'd never seen so much free standing candy in my life. It must've been a dream. Pallet after pallet of candy stacked ceiling high, row after row of Now & Laters. It was insane. I was literally salivating at the mouth.

I felt like I was in a Pavlov experiment. Every time the forklift would lower a pallet of Now & Laters, drool ran down my chin. We loaded the car down with more than $300 worth of penny candy. Once we arrived back at the store, kids noticed all the candy and began gathering around. I felt like a celebrity holding back the crowd, they were stand-ing in line just to see me. I removed all the Turtle candy from the display cases, with the exception of two boxes of turtle candy I put in my favorite hiding place for a midnight snack.

Mac was proud of his new since of entrepreneurship, he just sat behind a curtain in the back room and watch the kids feverishly buy up his candy. Some days he would sit be-hind the curtain eating candy as he watch me count out and sell the penny candy to school kids. Once his back was turned I pop a piece of candy in my mouth and washed it down with the orange soda that he gave me for slap boxing with another boy for his entertainment. Mac was a diabetic but he ate just as much candy as the kids that came into the store.

Although Mac never caused me any harm my mother was leery of him, she was leery of what he might teach me, some of his bad ways, how to curse and act out. I liked being around Mac because he was a character. Sometimes he'd sit quietly in his wheelchair with his head down while nibbling on a piece of candy. Unexpectedly he would yell out,

"Yee"

He slap the wheelchair twice on the handle, spin around in a circle and fire his gun twice into the ceiling. Then, he would slap the opposite arm of the chair, spin in the opposite direction and fire two more shots in to the ceiling then go back into a slump and continue eating candy.

I spent early mornings and long nights in the candy store selling penny candy to the neighborhood kids. My mother didn't mind that I spent so many hours working in the store because our house was but an eye shot from the front of the store. If my mother were to step out her yard to the sidewalk she could see the front door of the store. Every time I arrived home after work she questioned me as to what Mac told me that day.

I would never told her everything Mac said or did in the store, such as firing his gun into the ceiling while spinning around in his wheelchair. Once again I was working 12 hours a day only to receive nine dollars by the closing of the store. I would've appreciated it more if he paid me in candy. I wasn't too disappointed in the amount of pay I received because I made up the difference with two socks full of silver dollars and all the Now & Laters I could stuff in my pockets.

I was in the sixth grade and as luck would have it Larry was once again in my class, although this time he was inconspicuous and didn't cause much trouble, therefore; I did not mind his presence.

I sat quietly in the classroom and observed the girls in their granny dresses and all the boys with their Converse tennis shoes, displaying different color shoestrings while wearing at least three different pairs of tube socks. Being from a proletarian family my mother was reluctant to pay $15.00 for a new pair of Converses, so I took the lead from my brother. I tried to fix up my buddy El's **(tennis shoes that cost $1.99 with hard rubber bottoms)** by lacing the shoes up with two sets of shoestrings, red and white. This way, no one should know the difference. It didn't quite work out the way I had planned, not only was I laughed at in the classroom, I was laughed at on the school play ground as well. I couldn't take it anymore, so I asked my mother if she would buy me a pair of Converse (mother) "Boy are you crazy? I'm not going to spend $15 on a pair of tennis shoes".

That Saturday I took my hard-earned money, and caught the bus downtown. I was so excited, I could hardly stay in my seat. Within 10 minutes I would be sporting a new pair of Converses. The bus turned right off Meridian Street onto the downtown Circle and stopped in front of Murphy's. I pushed through the doors of the bus before they could open. I burst into the doors of Thomas Ands best known for carrying a wide variety of Converses. I walked into the store and it was like a dream come true, shelves and shelves of Converses, blue, red, white, and black. They even had the thick red, blue or white shoe strings that I'd always wanted, not the thin spaghetti strings that I laced my Buddy El's up with.

I meticulously took my time as I browsed the department store shelf by shelf, checking all the shoes but there was one small problem all the shoes were $15 each. There was only one pair under $15 and they were nine dollars and some change out the door, but the biggest problem was the shoes were one size too small. I was a size 8 and the shoes were a size 7. I snatched the shoes off the shelf and cradled them under my arm as though I was carrying a crate of Now & Laters. I continued to search the store for my size and a price that could meet my budget. I looked for an hour before surrendering to the fact that this was the only pair of shoes that I was going to get and I wasn't about to place them back on the shelf. I knew this was my only option but I also knew this fashion statement would hurt. I took all the money out of my pocket and place it on the counter. It was just enough money to pay for the shoes.

It didn't matter to me that I had to walk 3 miles home because I was ebullient by the new tennis shoes I just purchased. I carried one shoe in my hand as I walked down Meridian Street smelling the new rubber and playing with the shoe laces. I was so enchanted with my new shoes I didn't even realize I was standing in front of my house.

" (Mother)," Where have you been all this time?"

Mikey, I caught the bus downtown to buy some tennis shoes, and I didn't have enough money to ride the bus home so I walked.

(Mother) Boy your crazy".

I may had been crazy but I have my Converses just like everyone else. I could hardly wait till Monday, I was so excited I began prepping my clothes. I pressed out a pair of blue jeans and a shirt. I hung them over the back of the chair, then I laced my tennis shoes with red and white laces, I washed out two pairs of socks so that my shoes could keep a fresh smell.

Normally it would be a set back for me to walk from downtown but I was destined not to be the odd man out anymore. From now on I was going to be like everyone else with a freshly pressed pair of blue jeans, a white T-shirt and a brand-new pair of Converses. I lay in bed that night curled up with my new shoes next to my nose, smelling the new rubber and dreaming about the impression I would make on my friends. I jumped out of bed the next morning and slid into my freshly starched jeans. The jeans were as hard as boards. I had to do several squat thrusts just to loosen them up. I put on my freshly washed socks and squeeze my foot into my tightly fitting shoe. My shoes were so swollen from the thick socks and the small fit, my feet looked like two pumpkins, but I didn't care, because I had to be like everyone else.

I could hear my friends making their way downed the street approaching the front of my house, so I jumped over the fence striking a pose, displaying my new tennis shoes. "Oh man, those are nice Mikey". Smiling from ear to ear sucking up all the compliments, I joined the group and we walked to school, all of us wearing Converses with two sets of shoelaces and two pairs of socks. After one block of cruising down the street my feet began to cramp, my big toe started to bend in places I didn't even know it could bend. The closer I got to Mapleton Fall Creek School the more I noticed my feet were increasingly uncomfortable. My toes were going numb and my feet felt like they were in a vice grip. I dashed up the school steps and into the classroom.

I was just about crippled and couldn't take a step further as I slumped down on to the hard wooden and metal chair. I kicked my shoes off as though my feet were on fire. The circulation in my foot was cut completely off. My big toes looked like two large strawberries and my eyes were almost rolling to the back of my head from the pain.

I was too cool to display such pain in front of my peers, I couldn't let the rest of my classmates share in my embarrassing moment. They would never let me live down that I purchased a pair of shoes that were a size too small. I put my socks back on and slid my foot halfway into the shoe. Every time we changed classes, I put my shoes back on long enough to reach the other class, and once I was at my desk I took my shoes halfway off to give my toes breathing room.

I couldn't wait to get home. As soon as I walked in the door I had the bright idea of throwing my tennis shoes into the washer.

" Maybe this will loosen them up".

I thought to myself. Then I tossed them into the dryer, after 30 minutes of drying I was ready for the big test. I slid my foot into the shoe.

" Oh my god', I thought, these darn shoes must have shrinked two sizes"

"What am I going to do, I can't wear these to school.

My Buddy El tennis shoes lay in the back corner of the closet staring at me as though they were laughing. I was so mad and disillusioned by the shrinking of my converses I thought my buddy El's stuck its tongue out at me.

The next morning I was at a Mexican standoff with my new, fashionable Converse tennis shoes. I could envision the painful mile and a half journey to school and back home. Because of the numbing of my big toe the journey home seemed like a 5 mile walk. It was either be in pain and torment and be stylish or be comfortable and wear a dorky pair of tennis shoes. Style won the argument, so there I was once again walking up

Pennsylvania Street with swollen feet and tennis shoes that were now two sizes too small. I was so enamored with my feet, Mrs. Wright thought I was ignoring her Socratic method of teaching, so she called me to the chalkboard to write over and over again," I will pay attention in class". While all the students were dismissed for the day I stayed in the classroom to wash the chalkboard and pound the erasers together freeing them of chalk residue.

That Saturday I thought it will be a good idea to break in my new tennis shoes at the basketball court. Before we could get started playing all the teenage boys showed up taking over the court and forcing us to the sidelines. Lundy stood his ground refusing to leave the basketball court as ordered by the older boys. The game ensued but Lundy stood right in the middle the court shooting his basketball ignoring the older boys request. Out of nowhere came a 355 pound 6'3' tall man. He grabbed Lundy by the throat slamming him into the fence but Lundy refused to leave the court. He kicked, hit and punched Lundy repeatedly, finally grabbing Lundy's basketball throwing it across the street.

" Please just get off the court man, it's not worth it" I said.

Lundy ran across the street chasing after his basketball. Lindy was forced to stand on the sideline like the rest of us until the old boys finished playing the game.

We stayed at the park playing basketball late into the night. We left just before the street lights began to blink, we sat on Fred's porch looking at porn magazines and lifting weights until the Sandman sent everyone an opposite directions to their homes.

Talbot was a quiet street most of the time, the only noise you heard was the cheerful sounds coming from kids playing up and down the streets. Games like, hide and go seek, red rover, freeze tag, red light green light, hide and go get it.

Hi and go get it was my favorite game because it had a sexual connotation attached to it. Meaning if you found a girls hiding place she was yours to have for the night. I was too young to think about having any woman for my own, I was still playing with hot wheel cars and rocking socking robots.

The street light were our curfew. When the street light flickered, we were supposed to be in front of our house and when the street lights came all the way on everyone went into the house except for one exceptional family. I stirred out my bedroom window most nights, dreaming of foreign places I've never been. I often dreamed of California and walking along the sandy beaches, sitting in the shade of the palm trees and roller skating along the boardwalk. It was all a fantasy but for some reason I couldn't get it out of my head. I stared in the mirror at my face trying to imagine what I would look like once I turned 30 years old. Some people thought I was weird but it was early signs of my genius.

$\mathcal{T}$he Baby Fight

Summertime was quickly approaching, I could feel the surge of energy throughout the classroom, everyone seemingly mentally prepared to do nothing for three months but have fun, hanging out at the swimming pools and going to block parties. The last week of school was always fun, only a skeleton classroom was left during the final few days of school. I enjoyed this week because all we did was play throughout the entire week. I never got the privilege of missing the last week like other kids, my mother ensured that we stayed until the last day.

Summer had come and I was surely excited about the opening of Douglas Park and Riverside swimming pools, and the all night escapades of playing basketball with my four closest friends. I would awaken to find one of my friends Victor or Chris sitting outside my gate before I could brush my teeth and wash my face. Chris was a very creative and outgoing person. We spent our time building clubs and jumping ramps with our bicycles. When I was with Victor we spent our time relieving the grocery stores of their striped bubblegum or shooting someone in the neck with the BB gun.

Either way I was having fun. We would make our way down 29th St. on our way to Douglas park swimming pool we'd stop by the mailboxes and collect rubber bands to use for slingshots. Victor was a menacing kid but dangerously fun to be around. We made small changes in our plans for the summer each passing year, our old ways had not yet caught up with us. As time passed we matured from walking around with slingshots hanging out of our back pockets, to carrying BB guns. Someone who obviously didn't know Victor very well gave him a BB gun.

Since Victor and I were good friends he had no problem giving me a plastic bag of BBs and letting me keep the gun overnight. I was just as menacing with the BB gun as Victor, but the difference was I would shoot at cans and bottles. Victor shot at people. One day we were hiding on the side of Lundy's house behind some bushes that separated my yard and Lundy's yard. A group of kids were playing kickball across the street on the large paved asphalt parking lot.

Victor cocked the gun 10 times pumping pressure into the chamber. He aimed at the back of the kid's neck and squeezed the trigger, the kid jumped and turned and looked around as we slumped behind the bushes, laughing, covering our mouths trying not to give away our position. Victor passed the BB gun to me I cocked the gun 10 times, aimed at the back of the boy's neck, pulled the trigger, then missed. I cocked the gun once more, aimed the BB gun at the back of the boy's neck pulled the trigger and once again I missed. I gave the BB gun back to Victor. He then cocked gun once again, aimed at the back of boys neck and bull's-eye direct hit and off we ran down the alley to our freshly built clubhouse.

Our club house was an empty garage that was too dirty and too full of clutter to park cars in. So Chris, Eron, Johar, Victor and I cleaned up the garage with the permission of the home owner and used it for our own club. Once inside we would tie the door to keep out non-members or unwanted guest.

Later that evening Denton was standing in front of the house with his girlfriend as he normally did, hugged and kissing, while leaning against the fence. Marica and her boyfriend Carver were arguing on the front porch, at which time Marica was four months pregnant with Carver's baby. Carver decided he wanted to punch her out that day so he shoved her off the porch to the ground. Denton ran over to break to up the fight and then a fight ensued between Denton and Carver.

Denton pulled a box cutter from his back pocket and began cutting Carver across his arms, legs and face, anywhere he could hit him with the box cutter, slicing and cutting and twisting his hand to make sure the box cutter turned deep into the skin. Carver fled down the street and five minutes later he came back with plenty of help I've never seen before. Carver walked towards the fence and shoved Denton's head. Denton jumped over the fence and began his carving exhibition all over again.

Bryce drove up as Denton chased Carver a-crossed the street to the grassy field we played football on. Bryce jumped out of the car and removed the box cutter from Denton's hand. Denton was surrounded by at least 12 boys twice my size, but I wasn't going to let my brother get jumped by 12 guys so I ran into the house and grabbed the longest butcher knife I could find and shoved it into Denton's left hand. Once again in my opinion the fight was unfair, but once again Bryce removed the knife from Denton's hand, so I ran back into the house and took out a wooden cane that I been working on for the past couple of weeks. I went back outside and handed the cane to Denton. He only got two swings striking Carver on the head, shattering the cane into pieces. Bryce halted me steadfast from going in the house to get any more weapons. I watched as my brother and Carver fought heads up. Once the fight was over I went upstairs to console my brother. I couldn't help but to feel sorry for him as he nursed the open scrapes on the right side of his face.

I thought about the times he plotted to have me beaten up and yet he was the one the who ended up fighting. I never started a fight in my life, I've never had a reason to start a fight nor did I want to fight. I did what I had to when I was made to fight. I never fought because I want to prove I could beat someone, I only fought to protect myself.

The next day I noticed Carver walking down the street covered head to toe with bandages. He looked as though he had been in a car wreck. I've never seen one person with so many white bandages. One more bandage and he would've been considered the mummy. I didn't think much more about the fight that day, so I made my journey down the alley to my clubhouse where Eron, Chris, Johar, and Victor were already playing.

Routinely we tied a rope around the door knob onto a homemade latch anchor on the door frame, not allowing anyone in the front or back. We had the rope tied thoroughly around the door. Johar said that he had to leave and be right back. Three minutes later we heard a scuffle in the alley. Their must have been more than 10 teenage boys running down the alley headed towards our clubhouse. That's when it hit me, Johar had told them where I was. They began beating and banging all over the garage saying. "we are going to kill you when we get inside". They beat and banged on the door so frantically that the boards began shaking loose. The cans and candles that we had placed on the ledge for decoration had fallen to the floor, the boys behaved like a pack of wolves.

I was so afraid I climbed up into the rafters of the garage. Suddenly my sixth sense kicked in, I felt trapped. The bullies were so preoccupied with trying to knock down the back door of the garage. I frantically jumped from the rafters, 'quickly' I was able to get the rope off the door, then fled for my life. I jumped over 3 fences until I reached my backyard. Once again my guardian angels had protected me, for some reason, it wasn't meant for me to be pulverized. It wasn't meant for me to be kicked and punched, it just wasn't in the cards. The lively street of 29th and Talbot returned to its normal state, kids ran freely up and down the street playing freeze tag and hide and go seek. Weeks had passed deep into the summer and the fight between Denton and Carver was all forgotten. Marica reunited with Carver, aiding him to heal from his wounds, and Denton never defended her honor again.

I return to hanging out at the candy store with Mac. I hung around drinking sodas and waited on some of his customers. One afternoon a well poised, tall african-American man walked into the store. He was a delivery driver for Jessie potato chips. He walked in carrying four boxes of chips. His tall stature stretched up towards the sun, with his bald head glistening in the sunlight. One of his hands was three times the size of both my hands put together. He sucked down a soda as though he had a hole in the bottom of the stomach. He set the can on the counter and with one juggernaut swing the can was smashed thin as a quarter. I was so amazed I even considered joining his boxing club, but Riverside Park was at least 2 miles or more across town and more than a mile from my grandmother's home. My mother would never let me walk that distance alone.

A **neighborly ride to the grocery store**

By the time I was 17 I'd acquired my driver's license. I had been driving around six months, mostly running errands for my mother to the grocery store on capitol avenue or to the 7-Eleven on Fairfield Blvd. Either way, I didn't care. I just want to drive and be seen cruising around by all my friends who weren't driving yet. Friends of the family began to take advantage of my mother, asking her for rides to and from the store on a daily basis. My mother didn't have the heart to tell them no, so she shifted the responsibility to me. She knew that I had just gotten my license and I loved to drive. All of a sudden it was my responsibility to take all of her friends and friends of the family shopping and other places they wanted to go. I loved driving, I just didn't want to be trapped into sitting on the grocery store parking lot once again waiting for two hours.

One day I was told to take Rayford's girlfriend and her mother to the grocery store. I had to find a way out. After two hours of waiting on the parking lot, the two women emerged from the grocery store. Smiling from ear to ear after a successful Thanksgiving shopping trip, food almost spilling over the top of the cart.

I could not believe it, they just left their bags in the cart and sat comfortably in the backseat while I begrudgingly unloaded the cart into the trunk. I started the car, threw it in gear and slammed on the gas. The back of the car almost did a 180° spin before I could straighten out the wheel. I must've been going 80 miles an hour before I reached the first corner. I didn't even step on the breaks, I turned the corner making the back of the car fishtail around the curve. I looked in my rearview mirror both women were pinned to the back seat with their eyes bulging out of their heads. They thought for sure they were going to die that night.

I thought I heard a prayer coming from someone's mouth, but I didn't let up, as soon as I reached their street I slammed on the gas as I turned the corner. Before I knew it a police car was behind me flashing his lights. Now I was scared, slowly pulling over to the curb. I took out my drivers license and rolled down the window. Very timidly I asked.

"Is there a problem officer"?

The officer shone his flashlight in my face then asked for my registration. I opened up the glove box, felt around the loose papers for my registration, to my dismay my mother's 22 caliber pistol fell out of the glove box onto the floor.

I froze in position waiting for further instructions from the officer hoping he didn't see the gun lying at the tip of my fingers on the floor. I positioned my body trying to block the flashlight from shining on the gun, then I removed the registration from the glove box and handed it to the officer. He walked around to the back of the car and asked that I step on my break pedal.

Officer: " I didn't see your brake lights when you turned the corner, I wanted to make sure they were operating properly".

He handed me back my license and registration then went about his way.

I sat in the car with my head pressed against the steering wheel while the two women expediently unloaded their bags then ran into the house without uttering a word. I was mentally exhausted from the exchange with the police man, all I want to do was take the car back home and hand my mother her keys

$\mathcal{T}$he immaculate conception

I was now a sophomore in high school and had the envy of all of my freshman peers. I cruised the hallways of shortridge high school acting as a guide for the newly arriving freshman, 'the class of 1979'. It was refreshing to see my junior high school classmates finally arrive after standing behind a fence for an entire year waving as I passed by. We were all back together, ready and willing to live as young adults. Sophomores, juniors and seniors stood along the entry to the high school egging the freshmen on. "Fresh men, fresh men,! They yelled, laughing and clapping as the freshman filed into the school with apprehensive looks on their faces.

I couldn't help but enjoy the moment, I was an upper class man and very familiar with my surroundings. Sophomores, juniors and seniors didn't wear new clothes on the first day, but all the freshmen filed through the door wearing new blue jeans, patent leather shoes, and new Converse tennis shoes. The upper class-men wore clothes from the prior year, we had grown past wearing fancy outfits on the first day of school. Varsity football and basketball players strutted proudly up and down the hallways wearing their letter jackets. I played football in my sophomore year but not long enough to earn a letter. However, I did join the boxing club at Riverside and wore a Golden Gloves boxing jacket for my participation in my 1976 Golden Glove bout at Tyndale Armory. The school announced the results of my boxing match on the loudspeaker for everyone to hear.

I felt like I was in the prime time of my life. There were no more fights in school or after school. I was a captain and a platoon commander in the JROTC program. I met several young girls but none held my interest. Later in the school year I began dating Sarah Gatewood. She was tall, slim, quiet and unassuming. Her huge buck eyes pierced the side of my face as I turned the combination to my lock. Before I knew it I was walking her home from school on a daily basis. In the beginning our initial relationship didn't consist of much. I walked her home from school everyday, played around in the snow and had snow battles from the school to her front door. I was still very immature and had only been sexually active once in my life. I was 17 years old and very shy, not yet a man but ready to try.

I tried having sex once before, it wasn't a pleasurable experience and I was in no hurry to repeat it, but as fate would have it, Sarah was ready to take our relationship to the next level.

One day after school we walked our usual route home, playing in the snow, wrestling all the way to her front door.

"Come in quickly" she said.

Running to the bedroom taking her clothes off as She ran. I followed behind her as quickly as I could, by the time I reached her bedroom she was totally nude and lying in the bed.

"Get undressed, hurry up before my sister comes home" she said.

I disrobbed out of my ROTC uniform as quickly as possible and climbed into her bed. Two minutes later her sister walked in.

" Oh, oh, oh, I'm going to tell mama" she said.

We both jumped to our feet scrambling to get dressed. I ran into the front room carrying my ROTC shirt and jacket simultaneously pulling my pants up at the same time.

Sarah frantically tried frantically to calm her sister down, telling her we weren't doing anything. I sat in the front room trying to zip my pants up and put my shoes on. I kissed Sarah goodbye and ran down the street like a bullet train. Three days later I got a phone call, Sarah wanted to meet me by the bus stop after school. I didn't think much of it, I grabbed my books and gladly sat at the bus stop watching the pretty girls walk past walk out of the back door of Shortridge high school. Sarah arrived with a disgruntle look on her face. She looked down at the ground, and said.

" I'm pregnant".

Then, she hit me in the arm and walked off. I was totally flabbergasted, I was only 17 years old and didn't know what I was going to do with a baby. Within the next week Sarah began demanding that I take on the roll of a father. She forced me to take her to the uptown theater, saying, the baby wanted to see a movie. Once at the movies she said the baby needs nourishment, the baby wants popcorn, a large orange soda and a chocolate candy bar. I was broke as hell! I didn't have two nickels to rub together and this baby was already eating me out of house and home. I went into my emergency stash, a secret hiding place in my bedroom closet and retrieved my jar full of silver dollars and quarters. The uptown theatre only cost $1 per person. A large bucket of popcorn was $1.75 cent, orange soda was $1.50 cent and a candy bar was .45 cent.

It seemed as though she was using the baby to empty my secret stash. The following weekend she said she needed an engagement ring, so we jumped on the city bus and rode downtown to Woolworth's where I purchased her a $13.00 ruby ring. She was very pleased. As we walked down the street, she cringed onto my arm as if we had been married 100 years. I didn't know what to make of the whole situation, and I wouldn't dare breathe a word to my mother until Sarah's stomach began protruding from beneath her clothes and took all the guesswork out of whether she was pregnant or not.

I couldn't sleep a wink, I stayed awake thinking about the possibility of having another little person like myself running around the house. I couldn't believe I let myself get into such a die or need situation. I didn't take the time to put on a condom but how could I think about a condom, she was naked before I could get in the bedroom, and one thing for sure I wasn't going to turn it down with all her nudity in my face. Fortunately, I was able to get a momentarily mental break at the party Miss Appleton gave for all the kids in the neighborhood. Her daughters were my age and all of us attended the same school. Miss Appleton was a very nice lady and very proactive in giving the kids positive after school activities. Ms. Appleton's party was the biggest social event of our year, all the local girls would be there and fortunately for me the party was right across the alley from my mother's house. All I had to do was hop the fence, walk 30 paces and I was at the party. Of course a party wouldn't be a party without some form of alcohol, so a couple the boys purchased a bottle of Boons Farm wine to bring to the party.

We stood outside passing the bottle around is if we were adults, and to my surprise Sarah arrived with a group of friends. She walked past me as if I wasn't even there. She headed right down into the basement and jumped right into slow dancing with a boy we called Rook. Rook wasn't very smart. In fact he probably was the dumbest person I knew in up to that point in my life. Rook was notoriously known for dating girls much younger than himself, if the girl had a pacifier in her mouth, he wanted her. He was known for having sex with just about anyone, but unfortunately for me he was dancing with my girlfriend and to top it off he had a boner the size of Mount Rushmore.

I was half drunk but I knew a boner when I saw one. I stepped immediately between them.

"What the fuck is going on" I said.

Pulling her by the arm.

She reached back with one hand and slapped me so hard I thought I was shot.

" Is that the way to treat the father of your baby?" I said.

Refusing to let her arm go.

"I'm not pregnant, I got my period this morning" she said.

I didn't know what to think, but I knew I needed another drink, so I staggered back up the steps stumbling out of the basement and into the back yard. The boys were once again collecting .25 cent apiece to purchase another bottle of Boones Farm wine. I was more than happy to chip in. I wanted to celebrate my new found freedom from father-hood. Sarah and I went our separate ways but she kept my $13.00 ring, refusing to give it back or pay me $13.00. I didn't care because I was just happy to be single, free and childless. She transferred that year to another school and I was the happier for it. I no longer had to worry about bumping into her in the hallway or making unnecessary idle conversation just because I bumped into her. I was totally abdicated of all responsibility, and at last I was able to breathe again and be a 17-year-old boy.

The year moved on, by now Fred and I were full-fledged members of the Riverside box-ing team. We rode our bikes alone the scenic route of 30th St. As my Afro fluttered in the wind. A young thin girl sitting in her front yard called out to me. "Hey cutie, come here." I hastily stop my bike and made a U-turn in her direction, Fred continued on to Riverside Park. She jumped up and ran into the house leaving her cousins to answer for her.

"Why did she run in the house?" I said.

(Cousin) she's just shy, hey Lorraine, come back outside he wants to talk to you".

She walked her tall slim frame out of the house. She was tall and skinny, as thin as a rail. Her chest were flat as a board and there was no indentation of a butt to speak of.

Her most glaring attraction was her beautiful smooth skin and her long silky hair. A twisted braid seemingly endlessly hanging down her back passed her butt. I've never seen an African-American girl with such long beautiful hair, but she was mixed with another race. Lorraine was soft-spoken, she held her shoulders tightly squared as of her body was full of tension. She ground her teeth and wore her clothes as though she was practicing to be a lesbian. I found her pleasant to be around and a far cry from any of the girls on my block whom where loud, outgoing and vivacious. Everyday on my way to the boxing center I stop by her house and chat for 15 minutes, then off I went to Riverside boxing center to receive my daily beating.

My boxing coach was a professional fighter rated 10th in the Junior middleweight class by ring boxing magazine. My boxing coach loved the fact that I was a South Paw fighter. Meaning I was left-handed. In the boxing game most fighters had trouble adjusting to left-handed fighters. This was all the reason he needed to call me into the boxing ring every day to beat me into a new reality. Over the course of the year I developed a knockout punch using the boxing techniques I learned from him through osmosis. He really didn't have the time to train me, all I could do was assist him with preparing for his fights. One day his girlfriend came into the boxing center, she sat idly by the boxing ring observing him shadow box from one end of the ring to the other. I knew it wouldn't be long before I was summons into the ring. He wasn't about to let this opportunity pass. A chance to beat me senseless in front of his girlfriend, but I had other plans. For several weeks I was the first one at the gym. I practiced slipping punches, side stepping, moving my head to the right, allowing punches to slip over my shoulder, then I would shoot a power shot right down the center of the pike. I watched my boxing coach shadow box and spoil with other fighters, by watching him I was able to learn his timing and pick up on his rhythm. I stood outside the ring and observed how he threw his punch.

Every time he threw his punch I stepped to the right, then came back with a right cross follow by a left to the chin. I practice this move outside the ring unobserved to by himself. After three rounds at shuttle boxing he did just as I anticipated he would. "Hey Mike, glove up and get in the ring. He said, strutting around the ring waiting patiently for me to glove up. I stepped into the ring knowing it wasn't going to be another day of just being a human punching bag. The bell rang and we went immediately to it. His 12 ounce glove snapping in my face, slightly catching me on the chin. I wasn't worried, I knew I had his rhythm and his pace down to increments of a second. I knew what he was going to do before he did it.

After three minutes the bell rang giving us a one minute break. Fred cheer me on from the outside of the ring, causing Sammy to looked back over his shoulder at me with a puzzled look on his face. Sammy couldn't hit me, but how could this be, he was a professional fighter with a record of 18 wins and two losses. I was just an amateur who hadn't had my first fight yet. He angrily spit his mouth piece into the bucket, he was amazed that I could move out of the way of his punches. I turned with my back facing him so that he couldn't see I was smiling at Fred.

I knew he would come out a little faster and harder this time because he had something to prove. He had an audience of one, one girl with the promise of sexual fantasy if you could impress her with his boxing power. Sammy was rated 10th in the Junior middle weight class but rated as the 2nd hardest hitter in middleweight boxing next to Marvin Hagler. Little did his girlfriend know, I wasn't a professional fighter. I was just a kid who rode his bike 3 miles to the gym everyday just to be a living, moving and breathing punching bag for a professional athlete.

The bell sounded and we were toe to toe once again. And just as I thought, his punches came a little quicker a crisper. I was no longer able to move out-of-the-way of his snapping heavy handed jab. Everything he threw landed squarely on my chin but he could n't knock me out, which frustrated him to no end. He began putting all his weight behind his punches, then hitting me straight in the gut. I fell to the floor bent over spitting out my mouth piece.

" You okay boy, I told you to do bodywork" he said.

I eventually stood to my feet.

"Walk around the ring to catch your breath" he said.

He stood in front of his girlfriend leaning over the rope while she stroked his eagle. I took a deep breath, psychologically trying to prepare to go another round. I eventually got to my feet, just before the bell rang giving me a one minute break to shake off the cobwebs. After the break we were right back into it. His crisp snapping jabs were blinding. All I could see was a red glove coming towards my face then drawing back. He was hitting me so hard I was punch drunk before the second round ended.

 I believed he was frustrated that he could not knock me out. I was new to the game of boxing. I wasn't even a contender, but somehow my chin withstood everything he threw at it. I knew I couldn't take much more of this punishment, I had to focus on his rhythm and timing. I let him hit me with two clean shots to the head, once he got comfortable and felt she could hit me whenever he wanted I side stepped, slipping his punch. The punch flew right over my shoulder as planned. I responded with a right across over the top of his punch, then a straight left jab right down the pike. He stumbled back and fell onto the ropes, seemingly shocked by the power behind my punch. I was just as shocked as he, the bell sounded ending the three round sparring session leaving me the victor for a day. I didn't have many days like this in the ring. In fact this was the only day I nearly sat him on his butt. During the rest of my boxing sessions he pot shot me with stinking at his pleasure, leaving me bruised and wanting.

I saw myself in a different light. I knew I could take a lot of punishment but now I knew I could dish it out as good as I got. Boxing was fun but it wasn't something I wanted to make a career out of. I just boxed to get respect, and for some reason the boys in my neighborhood and at my school took their tough guy routine elsewhere. However, there was always someone who want to push the envelope and test my skills. My sister's boyfriend was ripe for the picking. He was a local neighborhood thug who lived off the repetition of his brothers. He wore his hat tilted back on his head, is Blue Jays were re-pressed and starched as stiff as boards. He wore wingtip Stacy Adams and walked as though he owned the world.

One day Victor and I was engaged in a boxing lesson on my mother's patio. In walked Herd, his hat tilted back on his head, smoking a cigarette. He flicked his cigarette to the side.

" Come on Victor lets box".

"Victor' "No" that's okay' Victor said, while handing the gloves to Herd. Herd put the gloves on. He wasted no time throwing lazy punches in my direction.

"Come on Mike let's go"

"Okay" I said.

At that moment a small crowd began gathering at the door. My mother and two of my sisters watched as the drama unfold. Herd through several lazy jabs barely nicking my chin. I knew I could knock him out whenever I wanted, my eagle was so inflated from the sparring session with my coach I knew Herd didn't have a chance.

He was so arrogant, throwing his punches and talking trash, I couldn't help but to teach him a lesson. He threw a lazy jab without much bite to it. I saw it coming from a mile away, I simply side stepped allowing his punch to fall over my shoulder. I came right back with a 1-2 jab knocking him for a loop. He covered his face and began staggering around the patio falling to the ground as though he was drunk. I quickly grabbed him keeping him from crashing embarrassingly to the ground. He wanted to continue but I suggested that he stop while he was ahead. Victor walked off laughing hysterically as Herd try to collect himself. He never challenged me to another boxing match and the story of that fight filtered throughout the neighborhood.

I continue my daily pilgrimage to the gym, five days a week for four hours a day of training. Everyday I stopped by Loraine's house, her next door neighbor was supposed to be some type of martial arts expert, he wore traditional kung fu outfits as well as shoes. He had an incredible kick but nothing else. However Fred did take karate lessons and earned a brown belt in tae kwon do. I could tell this kid never took a karate lesson in his life. However, I do believe he watched too many Bruce Lee movies and convince itself that he was professionally trained.

It wasn't long before Lorraine had us in a sparring session in her front yard. I must say his feet were very fast but I wasn't about to lose. I didn't use any of my boxing training but I did resort to some of the wrestling moves I learned in my gym class.

Once he kicked his foot in the air I simply went under his kick and body slammed him to the ground. He went home limping and I went into Lorraine's house and set on her couch draped with plastic. Her mother yelled from the other room.

"I'm going around the corner to the store, make sure that boy's gone when I get back".

"Ok" Lorraine said.

We set on the couch talking for 2 to 3 minutes and before I know it we were fully engaged in a lip lock.

"Let's go to my mothers bedroom" she said.

I was reluctant to do to go into the room but somehow the forces of nature put my feet in emotion. We struggled for five minutes trying to get into position but it was virtually impossible because she wouldn't take her pants all the way off. I finally surrendered to a sexless night and disappointedly went home. Lorraine called me after words saying that her entire family walked in the door just as I had left. Lorraine and I never became lovers, we stayed friends for the course of my short journeys to and from the gym, we grew in different directions and within a years time I would lose all contact with her.

My life wasn't all stalemate, after training for year I finally had my first boxing match. The Indianapolis Golden gloves boxing tournament held at the Tyndale armory. I walked whether than rode my bike to the center because I wanted to displays all negative or nervous energy festering in my mind. I slowly walked past Loraine's house, the house was normally teaming of life but for the first time the house seemed dark and abandoned. I took it as an omen and thought whether or not I should even go to the fight but I reluctantly kept moving forward. I knew nothing about boxing, or how to prepare for the fight or what to bring to a fight. My boxing trainer didn't tell me anything, we arrived at Tyndale Armory with a handful of boxing tickets, I didn't even know was available. I could have given them to my family or my ROTC director, Sgt. Woods who loved the boxing game.

I arrived at Tyndale Armory early, sitting in the back of the crowd I got to watch all the fights before mines. I was scheduled to fight the 15th bout out of more than 20 fights. 12 fights into the sequence I was summonsed to go into the locker room to have my hands wrapped and get dressed for the fight. I sat in the locker room getting my hands professionally wrapped, for the first time I felt like a real fighter. I was presented with a white and green boxing rope, a white pair of boxing shorts and a red, white and blue pair of size 12 boxing shoes. My feet were a size 9, the shoes flopped around on my feet like Bozo the clown. They slid the 12 ounce boxings gloves over my hands, ensuring my fingers were all the way to the top. They pull the laces tight, tying it in a double knot then securing the laces with a piece of tape wrapped around both gloves. Butterflies flattered freely of my stomach, I was a total nervous wreck. It would be my first time fighting in front of a crowd of 200 or more. People chanting my name as I walk towards the ring, my clown like shoes flopping on the floor in front of me, my non-color coordinated boxing robe and boxing trunks on display for all to see.

The boxing ring appeared to be lifted high in the air, three huge lights rested comfortably above the ring with smoke circling around the bulbs of lights giving a nostalgic feeling of the 1940s boxing era. I was in it now I thought to myself as I stepped in the sand box to the left of the steps, then making my way up the steps into the ring. The crowd was so loud I couldn't hear the instructions given by my boxing trainer. People were yelling my name by the hundreds but I was a nervous mess and all I could see were mouths moving, muted by the butterflies in my stomach.

The bell rang and out we came. The first punch was straight to the stomach, a hard jab to the stomach that I was not ready for. I cringed and fault the rest of the round with my right arm covering my stomach. Larry took very advantage of the situation and consistently shot left jabs to my lip. Before the first round was over, my lip was split right wide open.

"You have to do something, you just can't keep taking a beating, you got the power let your hands go." My trainer said.

The bell rang for the second round, I knew I was in trouble, I had to find away to work against his rhythm. So I settled in, I let him shoot jabs to my lip. After the third jab I was able to get his rhythm. I side stepped allowing his place to go over my shoulder. The next jab I caught with my right hand, flung it out of the way hitting him squarely in the eye with a left cross. He hopped and staggered across the ring, grabbing his eyes. The referee jumped in front of him holding him by his head to examine his eye. The doctor was called into the ring to determine whether Larry could continue the fight. Blood gust profusely from his eyes while they rush to stop the bleeding.

The fight would have been stopped but Larry was to far ahead on the scorecards, so they allow the fight to go into the third round. By the third round I was so tired I could barely walk to my corner. I regret the times doing training I would take a shortcut across the park instead of running the entire 4 miles. It was a lesson learned and I vowed to never take shortcuts while training again. Larry won the fight that night, and several years later he went on to be rated number 10 in ring magazine in the Walter weight division. I fought several more times before quitting the gym, boxing wasn't my first love or passion, it was just something I did to fill the empty void in my life.

Olive Oyl

Boxing was fun but I needed money. It seemed like all the other boys in my school had money except for myself. I was tired of being broke. I was badly in need of new shoes and clothes. The empty spaces in my pockets screamed for relief and to make things worse Rayford suggested that I didn't ask my mother for money. He said, she was having a tough time and needed a break. But my shoes were in disrepair and I definitely needed a new pair because my shoes didn't have much milage left in them. One day I arrived home from school and found two brand-new pairs of shoes tucked right under my bed. Rayford took it upon himself to buy me two pairs of shoes. I couldn't believe it, and the next week he informed me about a job at Saul subway.

I ran over to Saul subway as if I had won the lottery. I stood outside Saul's Subway for a brief second, trying to compose myself and catch my breath. The restaurant was choked with customers, waitresses busy serving drinks by the hundreds. Dishes piling up in the tubs located in the waitress bus stations. Within seconds I was put to work bussing dish tubs to the kitchen, and cleaning off tables. I was sent upstairs to prepare the kitchen for night dinning. So I shot upstairs into the dining part of the restaurant called the attic. I fired up the dishwasher. While waiting for the dish washer to fill I grabbed a slice of chocolate mousse pie from the freezer, slouched back comfortably against the dishwasher and began porking the pie down my throat. Once I had my shot of sugar I started preparing julienne salads until the salad prep girl arrived.

The salad prep girl's name was Eileen, she was a 6 foot tall, slim white girl. She wasn't very attractive, in fact she was kind of homely. I thought she resembled the character from the Popeye cartoons; Olive Oyl. Her body was flat as a surfboard, she had an unassuming nature, with a nondescript personality. She only spoke when she was spoken too. I believed she was borderline developmentally delayed or she was a dull normal. There was something about her looks that was unescapable, she was soft spoken and had a delicate touch. She moved very slow but was very meticulous in the way she wield her knife, slicing every bit of the cucumber as if there was an intentionally diabolical purpose to the way she made each cut.

She applied excessive pressure on the knife and with every cut she ground her teeth. Somehow she was able to reveal the softer side of her enigmatic personality. She piled salad on the plate, undulating in her movement, placing freshly cut cucumbers and boiled pickled eggs and generous strips of ham on top of the lettuce. Yellow onions were used to intensify the flavor. Croutons covered the rest of the plate, to enhance the size of the plate making a common salad into a thing of artistic work. It wasn't long before I was summoned to go down stairs and prepare four trays of rosin potatoes. I wrapped each potato in aluminum foil, placing 25 to 30 potatoes on four metal cooking sheets, then setting the oven at 350°. I slid the sheets into the oven. It took me about 30 minutes, 30 of the longest most uncomfortable minutes of my life. I was totally creeped out by the stories of other employees being bitten by rats as large as my foot. I even witnessed large ghetto rodents running freely under the tables, eating the droppings of food left by the rich patriot pigs.

To put it another way, the customers were mostly upper-middle-class professionals and it appeared that they didn't care about the condition which they left the tables and floors or the cleanup that would follow. All they wanted to do was gorge themselves with succulent steaks prepared by uneducated would-be chefs from the ghetto one block over from the restaurant. They porked out on the rosin baked potatoes topped with sour cream and chives, unknown to themselves prepared by a dish washer. The restaurant was famous for its food, often patronized by doctors, lawyers and anyone else of prominence in the city.

I made it my business to cruise around the restaurant in between picking up dish tubs from various stations, I watched the customers and secretly listened to their conversations. I mostly enjoyed talking with Olive Oyl. After six hours working together she began to open up and allow me to enter her cucumber cutting developmentally delayed world. I couldn't help but to listen closely as she laid her life story at my feet. She said she had been raped two years ago by an African American male and since that time she had been trying to find him to force him to be a father to their 2 year old daughter. She talked nonstop for an hour, I passively listened as she pontificated on and on. The longer she talked the more twisted and perverted her story got. She loathed the ideal of searching for her rapists but she felt it was necessary to let him know that he fathered a child.

During her time off she would cruise up and down Indiana Avenue, the last place she saw her assailant. After three hours of walking their he was mindlessly leaning against a concrete building without a care in the world. She confronted him without accusation only with a handful of baby pictures. She beseeched him to come see his daughter but he chuckled to himself with a condescending smile then escorted her to what she thought was his apartment. Instead it was just another vacant building, not as much as a mattress on the floor. He proceeded to rape her once again. I couldn't help but feel pity for Olive Oyl because even after telling me this sad story she punctuated it with.

"I'm going to keep looking for him until he accept his role as the father of my child".

I began to develop a bad taste and disliking in my mouth for Olive Oyl. When she finally stopped talking I could see the light bulb turn on in her head. At that moment she invited me over to her house but I demurred because of the possibility of our spending the night together. I didn't want her to divulge anymore depressing stories of her life.

I tried to stay out of the kitchen and made it a point to hang out around the bus tub stations, I only went into the kitchen when it was absolutely necessary because I didn't want this woman to soliloquize herself around me anymore. By this time I was tired and pretty much done for the day. My shoes were soaking wet and my fingers looked as though I had been in water for 12 hours. My clothes smelled of corned beef and my pockets occupied empty spaces where tips would normally fill those gaps. I didn't vociferate about the tips that were promised to me by the waitress hours earlier. I was a dish washer and a busboy, therefore; I only bussed tables at the waitress request, but the request was supposed to come with tips at the end of a shift. One waitress stepped forward and gave me three dollars for bussing 10 tables that were shoved together for a birthday party.

I was young, but I wasn't that young, I wasn't going to put up with the BS. Therefore, I was forced to create my own rules about tipping, and the percentage I deserved. If the customer left $10 I took $2. I didn't enjoyed taking tips but they forced my hand. After cleaning several tables and not being tipped by the waitress I no longer felt guilty about forcing my own tip.

Sunday morning, I was at work for the evening shift which began at 3 PM. The deli and the dining room section of the restaurant were closed for the day because prohibition laws still apply in Indiana on Sundays. No one was allowed to sell liquor anywhere in the city, but somehow the alcoholics and the obsessive drinkers would find adventure in seeking out club owners that would risk their licenses and their business to sell a six pack of beer at twice the price out of the back door of the bar. I couldn't believe people would go through this much trouble just to have a beer because the law said you can't have one on Sunday.

No one ever thought it would be just as easy to buy the liquor on Saturday and put it away to drink on Sunday. Maybe people didn't do that because it would take all of the fun and suspense out of the game. In the meantime I was stuck at work on Sunday, baking potatoes in a rat infested restaurant, looking at my feet and around the machines to ensure that no rats were biting on my shoes. I wrapped those potatoes quick fast and in a hurry, as if I was in a potato wrapping contest. I was totally creeped out, the kitchen was dark and spooky. I took every shortcut possible to get out of the kitchen as quick as I could. Once the ovens were set and the potatoes were baking I'd sneak around to the bar in search of an open liquor bottle or beer tap. Instead I found a bag of lay's potato chips and an open soda dispenser.

I placed my mouth under the Coke tap and drank soda like a horse drinking from a water trough. I was in hog heaven until I felt something squirm over the top of my foot. I threw the chips in the air, jumped over the bar and scurried outside to the sidewalk. Just as my feet hit the pavement two young girls were strolling by, I wasn't really interested in them I just didn't have anything to do at the moment, so I persuaded them to come back and talk to me. They kept walking when I called to them, I didn't give up I yelled at them two more times before they turned and began walking in my direction.

One was tall and fair skinned with an awesome figure, the other one was small quiet and reserved, her face was covered partially with a bonnet hat and I could barely get a glimpse of what she looked like. The tall light skinned girl was more of my type. I through out my best lines but after two minutes of talking she mentioned she was dating one of my friends. I didn't want to come up empty handed, therefore; I shifted my conversation to the quiet and reserved one. I didn't care for her at first but she slowly grew on me. I was partially attracted to her because she was soft spoken and appeared to be a very gentle person.

I was loath to give her my phone number because of the crazy cucumber cutting bitch upstairs who was also quiet and unassuming but was prated underneath it all. Cindy and I talked over the phone for the next couple of weeks although I was still technically involved with May. May and I began to drift apart spending less and less time together. Every time I saw her she spoke of moving to Arizona to go to college. We ended our relationship on that note, the day after our high school graduation we went our separate ways. Cindy and May were two extremely different personalities. Cindy was good at math and was very focused on doing well in school, she wanted things in life and was willing to work hard to achieve her goals.

I would sat with her and write out math problems just for the fun of it but there was something mysterious about her that I just couldn't put my finger on. In the meantime her ignorant jackass of a brother would interrupt my thoughts by trying to show how tough he was by bullying his friend Jeff, yelling absurdly close in his face and making threatening comments about hurting him physically. I just ignored his dumb antics as well as his dumb comments. He even tried to cajole Jeff to start a fight with me to enter-tain his sick little twisted mind.

He was a true pain in my butt and I was sure we would lock horns in the foreseeable future. Cindy had four brothers and two younger sisters. They lived in a large rat infest-ed wooden double with three bedrooms on each side. The couch was fitted with the traditional plastic covering that no one would dare sit on in fear of falling asleep and de-hydrating to death. Cindy's mother was a very light skinned women closely resembling someone of the white persuasion. She was a country girl from Mississippi with tell-tale signs of Mississippi culture in her behaviorism.

She wore a gold tooth in the middle of her mouth that was hard to miss because of her infectious smile. She had a way of luring men into her sinister web, destroying mar-riages along the way. She even had a theme song (clear up women) sung by Betty Wright. She would repetitiously play the same song 24 hours a day until the needle on the record player was worn down and no longer usable. I sat quietly in the living room and watched her dance around in a circle with a glass of liquor in one hand and a half smoked cigarette in the other. She was the cliché of her time. I tried not too attract at-tention to myself but Cindy's sister sat atop the staircase and shot paper spit balls through a straw onto my Afro.

I alerted Cindy to the situation, before I knew it, Cindy ran to the top of the steps and dragged her sister down the steps by her hair.

"Say you're sorry!"

With her foot on her sister's neck, pulling her hair with her right hand, making her apologize before striking her in the back with her fist, then shoving her toward the staircase whining. This was a side of Cindy that I had not yet seen since it was early in our relationship, but I did notice she could go from 0 to 80 in less than 10 seconds flat then back to zero as if nothing ever happened. It seemed as though the house was always packed with people or people constantly running in or out, taking bites of food here and there, eating on the run then back in streets. This was a very unpredictable place, I never knew when we would get a moment of peace to ourselves.

In the month of April my girlfriend Cindy and I were sitting idly on the couch. Cindy's legs were stretched across my lap, her back resting comfortably against the arm of the couch. We sat around talking while I massaged her feet, purposely hitting the points that would sexually arouse her.

Her brother came back in the room and said.

"What the hell is going on here."

He reached down and grabbed Cindy by the arm snatching her off my lap. But to his surprise my pants were zipped up and securely fastened. There wasn't any sign of fornication. He looked at both of us with an evil eye, made a moaning sound then walked back out the front door eating his baloney sandwich. Cindy sat next to me smiling, she laid her head on my shoulder, stuck her hand out and asked for her five dollars. I whispered in her ear.

"I'm still erract".

She laughed, jumped up and sashayed toward the front porch as her brother Robbi walked back and forth peeking in the window.

I cleaned myself up the best I could and reluctantly walked outside on the porch and sat ten feet away. Cindy and I were smiling and laughing to ourselves, as if we had gotten away with the perfect crime. Robbi leaned heavily against the frame of the front door cutting his eyes back and forth at both of us while he continued to devoured his dried up baloney sandwich. I was done dealing with this asshole, I had pressing business elsewhere. So I leaped from the pouch, waved farewell to Cindy then made my way back across the bridge toward my mothers house. I couldn't help but to pass by Sabrina's house. She was the prettiest girl in school but there was one small problem, she didn't brush her teeth. I'd never seen that much food caked up on someone's teeth. I didn't understand how a girl so pretty could miss the most vital part of her conversation piece, her mouth. I thought it was a fluke the first time I saw her, but she was this way every time we talked. Teeth caked over as if she had not brushed for months. I had no time for yuck mouth, so I made my way down two blocks to the park on 29th and Talbot.

I was in luck there were two boys playing a game of 21. After playing for 10 minutes we changed the game to a game called booths. Who ever had the lowest score at the end of the game gets kicked in the butt by all the other players. The rules were, we could only kick the person with the side of our foot. The game got under way, I played harder than I ever had played before. Victor was the best player and a natural shooter so I tried to keep up with him making basket for basket. The other guy fell far behind on points, I smiled and stepped out of the way as Victor easily ran by me and landed the ball in the hoop making the final point of the game. Victor told the other kid.

" Well, you lost. Lean on the fence".

The kid did what Victor asked, placing both hands on the fence. I went first, and did just as the rule said, I kicked him with the side of my foot. Victor got a running start from 20 feet, he ran fast as he could and kicked the boy with the point of his foot as though he was trying to kick him to the Moon.

The boy must've jumped 50 feet in the air clutching his butt on the way up and falling to the ground in agonizing pain. Victor laughed and ran through the sandbox climbing over the concrete castle and the other obstacles on the playground trying to escape the screaming young boy chasing him around the park clutching his butt with one hand, seemingly in utter pain. I couldn't help but to laugh at the spectacle before me, although I did feel sorry for the young boy, but he knew the situation before getting involved in the game.

He knew Victor was not going to honor the terms of the game and use the side of his foot. This wasn't his first time he had been tricked by Victor. One day we were playing football in the big field across the street from my house. Victor kicked the ball to the young boy then pretended like he was going to let him run by and score a touchdown. Once the boy got side-by-side with Victor, Victor stuck his arm out and clothes lined the young boy making him flip in a complete 360°circle, then took off running down the street laughing. Everyone on the block knew Victor and the type of stunts he pulled. Victor was the most naturally athletic person I have ever known. He could catch and throw a football with little effort. Lundy and Ray had an arm for throwing a football as well, but never pursued or developed their gift. My only talent was in my hands 'Boxing'. But I didn't have much time anymore for tomfoolery. I had an appointment too meet with a Marine recruiter that evening.

I felt my life was at a stalemate and graduation from high school was just around the corner, I knew there would come a time I would have to leave my mother's house and make it on my own. I was so excited, I could smell my emancipation in the air. I was mentally exhausted thinking about paying my own rent, utility bills, car payment and other life changing chores adults were supposed to do to survive. I was scared out of my mind at the possibility of failing the ASVB exam for the second time. I knew I had to change my methods of study if this was going to become a reality, so I acquired four pages of word knowledge covering front and back of the page.

I sat in my room for three days, not going down the street to play basketball, not hanging out with Cindy or spending time with my friends. All I did was study and pray until I knew the list back and forth. In between study times I would stand in the mirror and imagine myself wearing a set of dress blues, the white hat with a black brim flank by gold buttons on both sides, placed squarely on my head, the high collar with two gold Marine Corps emblems, then all of a sudden my chin was squared and I was a Marine.

My only focal point at that time was becoming a United States Marine, nothing else mattered not even my high school diploma or the fact that I was leaving my hometown and people that I loved behind. I wanted to be challenged, I wanted to see if I could stand on my own 2 feet and take what ever the corp could dish out. Growing up without a father created a huge gap of uncertainty in my mind. I questioned everything I did, right down to the smallest detail. I was never sure that I was making the right decision about anything because I wasn't taught to think outside the box. Everything I learned, I learned from the streets and the people I associated myself with. However, my mother did teach me how to respect others and things that belonged to other people. My mother never overly indulged me, I received the basic needs: shoes, clothing, food, and a roof over my head. Learning how to become a man I had to learn from examples in my small enclave.

All the men in my life spent their time chasing women. If they weren't chasing women they were getting drunk at a local bar on Indiana Avenue, or planning a scheme to get some sort of ill-gotten gains. I never saw an example of a man going to college or raising a family. The closest I came to seeing a man working at a steady job was my stepfather. He would get up at four in the morning, go to work then come home sloppy drunk at 10 PM. He'd sat at the kitchen table eating dinner, then stagger upstairs, walking right past me not saying a word. Once up stairs he would flop down on the bed and pass out.

He was the most direct example in my life that I had of what a man did on a daily basis. I did not know any better because I didn't have any better examples. I did have an uncle named George who worked at Regen's bakery, and I'm pretty sure he went to work everyday on time for 30 years, and at the end of working 30 years the bakery told him to piss off, not giving him retirement. He and his wife Dorothy, always had the newest cars in the family. They had a small, dainty two bedroom house with plastic covering the couch and chairs. I found it odd that my auntie was a school teacher, yet her husband couldn't read a word, but he was good with his hands and could build almost anything as well as being an excellent mechanic. I do believe he would've been a good role model but I only saw him once every five or six months when he came by our house with a box of stale donuts trying to put a smile on our faces. Sadly, I was no longer a little kid. I was 18 years old and a box of stale glazed donuts wasn't going to change the dynamics of my life in the next two months. My father would occasionally sat in his car parked in front of our house. I could see in his face he wanted our love but I was so disenfranchised from the father son relationship I'd walked past his car with looking in his direction. He was too late, I was raised without the aide of a father. I chose my parental representatives like I chose my candy, 'with purpose'.

My life would change drastically in the next month . I was growing as a person and this path that I had chosen I must walk alone. Later that day I made my way to the Afee station where more than 50 other individuals of different ethical backgrounds and genders were all taking the same test but for different branches of the service. I was very proud to be one of the few in the room that was taking the Marine Corps exam but in hindsight I was one of the few idiots that was taking the Marine Corps exam. I finished the exam and was escorted into the other room. Anyone that failed the exam was shown the door.

I was so excited I couldn't hold it inside. I told everyone, even the people on the bus. I ran down 29th and Talbot as though I won the lottery. Once I approached my front door, I stopped. I walked in as cool as a glass of water in the summer time. I sat at the kitchen table, crossed my legs and grabbed a section of the newspaper. My mother stared at me as she stirred her Folger's coffee.

"Where have you been all day"? She asked.

"I was at the recruiting station, I took the Marine Corps exam and passed it, my departure date is July 18."

My mothers eyes got big and suddenly she stopped sipping her coffee and began haranguing me about the Corps.

"Why in the hell did you join the Marines? Are you crazy?"

"I want to be tested, I want to know who I am and if I could stand on my own two feet, this is something that I must do alone. "

"I hope you know what the hell you're doing". She said.

"Well, if I don't were going to find out July 18".

So back up stairs I went. I couldn't sleep a wink. I swear I must have been awake for five days straight. I pretty much kept to myself other than occasional visits to Cindy's house and our well planned 7 PM trips to Riverside Park where I parked, turned off the car, turned on the radio, then climbed in the backseat where the seduction began. I was no stranger to the Riverside Park area because I was on the Riverside boxing team and I dated two young girls in the area the year before. I think Cindy liked all the personal attention I was giving her. We stopped at White Castle, picked up a 10 sack and two chocolate shakes, we threw our feet up on the arm rest of the front seat and choked down our White castle hamburgers until one of us let out a raunchy fart or belch.

We had gotten very comfortable after stuffing ourselves with hamburgers, so we took off our shoes and unbuttoned our pants at the waist to let our stomachs stretch freely. I realize we had forgotten about the time, three hours had passed and my mother had to be at work within an hour so we began scrambling around on the back floor trying to find our shoes. All of a sudden it hit me she doesn't know I'm moving 2500 miles away. I may as well move to the moon, because the Corp doesn't allow phone calls until the 10th week of boot camp. I dropped Cindy at her door then off to the gas station to replenish the tank, arriving home just in time to hand the car off to my mother. I stood on the side walk watching her turn the corner on 30th St. I went one house down the street and plopped down on the steps with my friends, where we sat outside until 12 midnight when the street lights began flashing, then off we all went to our separate homes.

I stayed up late that night, wide awake staring out my bedroom window, my mind was going 100 miles an hour searching for an answer about my future in the military and where I would be five years from today. I couldn't help but wonder how my mother sustained herself and eight children all these years. I could barely stomach the fact that I would be expected to support myself from this day forth. It scared me to death because I had always been under my mother's roof, eating my mother's food, wearing the clothing she brought. All of this would come to an end in less than 45 days. I'd be reluctantly cut free of the apron strings.

It had been a month since I enlisted in the Marines and still I could not muster the courage to tell Cindy. So I just let it ride until that one fateful day. Tiana, Denise, Herb and I were playing cards in the front room. The rules were if you lost a hand you had to drink a glass of water, everyone was willing to comply with the rules except Tiana. Tiana lost a hand and refused to drink the water. I obliged her by pouring a tall glass of water and placed it in front her.

Tiana said "I'm not drinking the damn water".

I told her

"But you lost, it's the rule, everyone drinks water when they lose and you know you better drink the water like everyone else".

She still refused, so I grabbed the pitcher of water sitting at the opposite end of the table and tossed it in her face, then jetted up the steps to my room and locked the door.

Denise and Herb uncontrollably laughed which enraged Tiana even more. She ran up the steps behind me screaming my name and cursing like a drunken sailor. I was quick to slam the door in her face while laughing on the other side of the door which infuriated her more. She began kicking and hitting my door profusely with her fist. She stood there soaked as though she accidentally fell in a swimming pool. She pounded, screamed and kicked on the door until she realized it was of no resolve so she grabbed my brand-new pair of white Converse and flung them outside in the mud, giving my German Shepherd something to chew on. I was so pissed off I ran into her bedroom, grabbed her favorite nightgown, tied it in a knot, dipped it in the toilet then flung it on the roof next door. Tiana ranted and whined until my mother forced me to get a stick and get the nightgown down from the roof and Tiana was forced to retrieve my shoes from the back yard and clean them off. I ran off down the street to the park while Tiana stood outside fuming over the incident and cursing my name as I ran to the basketball court for a brief game of 21. I soon was crossing the bridge on 25th and central to Cindy's house.

As I approached, there was a crowd standing on the front porch, her brothers, sisters, mother and stepfather. I could see something was amiss, and it made me very uncomfortable as I approached the porch. Cindy turned her back towards me as I stepped on the porch then ran into the kitchen and pretended as though she was cooking, at that moment I know Tiana had called and informed Cindy about my enlistment in the Marines. Cindy wanted nothing more to do with our relationship and wanted to move her life in a different direction then the path I had chosen, so I walked away with an Erie feeling in my stomach as if someone had kicked me. A month and a half later I was being picked up by my Marine recruiter at 9 AM in the morning to be transported to the recruiting station for final processing and a flight to San Diego, California. My mother and I stood outside that morning waiting for the recruiter to arrive. As usual he pulled up in a little ford escort with the Marine Corps emblem on side.

I began dragging the seabag toward the car.

The recruiter said "Where are you going with that?"

"I said "To boot camp"

Recruiter: "You don't need that, I just need you".

So I gave the bag back to my mother and hopped in the front seat of the recruiter's car. As the car drove away my mother stood in the front yard watching me drive off teary-eyed with a slight lump in her throat, however; she did summon enough strength to wave a final goodbye. I stared at her out the window until the car turned the corner onto 30th Street. I barely caught a glimpse of her struggling to drag the seabag back up the steps into the house. I scanned the neighborhood with my eyes hoping to catch a glimpse of someone I knew so I could wave goodbye to them but no one was around. It was as if the streets were purposely empty. No one saw me leave. There was no one there to say good luck or I'll see you when you get back. It made me feel empty, unloved and alone. For the first time in my life 29th and Talbot was empty, there wasn't a soul to be found, everyone had disappeared into their own lives and I was on my way to a new reality. There were a lot of first for me that day. The first time I've flown on a plane, the first time I would visit California, the first time I would feel what it was like to miss my mother and the first time I would miss someone that I cared deeply about. The most significant thing of all, I was leaving as Mikey but I would return a Marine.

I would like to dedicate this book to all the young man and women that I grew up with.

All the young men or women that live on.
Hillside Street,
30th & Park Avenue,
30th & Delaware Street,
29th & Talbot Street,

School #38 autobahn, the Christian center, School #60, Mapleton fall Creek, School #76, Shortridge high school.

And a special thanks to my mother, for being an awesome provider.

Pray that I live and celebrate all those who made a difference of my life. Each person added it a different ingredient in my life and for that I am eternally grateful. I only hope that you read, love and enjoy this book and may it become a personal part of your Library collection.

To my family and closest friends may God bless you in Heaven as he is blessing me on earth.

Dorothy and George Wallace
Carol Gray
Sonny Sheldon
Ruben & Estherline Shelton
Mattie Horney
Raymond Gray Senior
William Gray
Norman Gray
Frank and Onetta Vaughn
Sherry Gray

Dalbert Gray

Kenny Ross

Mr. and Mrs. Knox

Estherline and Ruben Sheldon

Kim Crumes

Billie King

Ray Burton

Warren Patterson

Cynthia Clark

Peair Freeman

Mac

Rose

Mr. and Mrs. Jenkins

Bay Alexander

Tinker

Carton Waters

Willie Williams

Janetta Riddick

GW Flemons

Jerry Crane

Eddie Nance

Robert Clark

Nathan Alexander

Anna and Vicki Fruit Quake

Michael Luke

June bug Kamp

Ms. Kamp

May you travel at Gods speed.

www.ingramcontent.com/pod-product-compliance
Lightning Source LLC
Chambersburg PA
CBHW060254290526
45789CB00001B/323